D1365532

Total Quality Management for Schools

HOW TO ORDER THIS BOOK

BY PHONE: 800-233-9936 or 717-291-5609, 8AM-5PM Eastern Time

BY FAX: 717-295-4538

BY MAIL: Order Department
Technomic Publishing Company, Inc.
851 New Holland Avenue, Box 3535
Lancaster, PA 17604, U.S.A.

BY CREDIT CARD: American Express, VISA, MasterCard

Total
Quality
Management for Schools

LEO H. BRADLEY, Ed.D.
Associate Professor, Educational Leadership
Xavier University, Cincinnati, Ohio

TECHNOMIC
PUBLISHING CO., INC.
LANCASTER · BASEL

Total Quality Management for Schools
a **TECHNOMIC** publication

Published in the Western Hemisphere by
Technomic Publishing Company, Inc.
851 New Holland Avenue
Box 3535
Lancaster, Pennsylvania 17604 U.S.A.

Distributed in the Rest of the World by
Technomic Publishing AG

Printed in the United States of America
10 9 8 7 6 5 4 3 2 1

Main entry under title:
  Total Quality Management for Schools

A Technomic Publishing Company book
Bibliography: p. 209
Includes index p. 211

Library of Congress Card No. 92-61824
ISBN No. 0-87762-972-2

To Mom, always at my side, regardless.

CONTENTS

PREFACE

It has been said that perception is truth. The perception of many people outside the educational community is that education is in need of reform. This is due largely to the impression that schools are not producing the educational results that are necessary for the current and future needs of this country.

To this continuous cry for change from the public, schools have basically responded with more of the same. Changes and innovation are constantly pursued by schools and other related organizations, but they have been mainly transitional in nature. Schools have not moved very far off center. The school reform that has been implemented has held on to most of the past while pursuing cautious innovation. Basically, schools have attempted to fit change into the existing governance and educational structure.

This book deals with substantive change. It does not call for transition, but for a transformation. This transformation involves governance, curriculum, instruction, staff development, assessment, and leadership. The proposals of this book are a daring departure from the past practices of schools. That is the strength of the book. It does not give "more of the same" solutions or strategies with a new coat of paint.

However, the content of this book has a rational base in both theory and practice. The idea of schools based on quality is fermenting throughout both society and the educational community. The pursuit of quality as the best means of making this country competitive and productive in a global market is permeating both the private and public sector.

Organizations, institutions, and industries are basing their future survival on quality in products and services. This book is based on these efforts, many proven by statistical results, and others accepted in management circles as solid practice.

Although quality has not yet been accepted in educational circles to the extent that it is being embraced by private and public enterprise, the school reform literature abounds with talk of the need for more part-nerships with the customers and clients of education, and the notion of students as workers, not as passive recipients of instruction.

It is my fervent hope that this book will serve as a catalyst for the idea that schools must be client-based, therefore quality-based, and that the transformation that this requires will move schools forward into substantive changes. These changes will challenge the social and political perception that schools are a closed system, unwilling or unable to meet the challenges of its client systems.

ACKNOWLEDGEMENTS

First of all, I would like to thank my brother Jean for first introducing me to the concept of quality control in 1957, my senior year in high school. He probably didn't think I was listening. Thirty-three years have passed since then. But I've never forgotten his prophetic words, "quality is the wave of the future."

I am also deeply grateful to the managers in the private sector who not only gave me their time and expertise, but showed a genuine interest in my research and work. I think they are representative of the public's desire to help schools improve. Their names are contained in the footnotes and bibliography.

A lot of credit for the format of this book should go to Leo Motter of Technomic Publishing Company, Inc. His feedback was invaluable in controlling the manuscript and fitting the parts together. He was a master at abandonment.

Last of all, thanks to Katherine Keough for her support, and to two great typists, Ida Bickel and Karen Shaw.

THE MEANING OF QUALITY

The chapters of Part One are based on both primary and secondary research. Secondary research was used to determine operational definitions, rationales, history, and derivation for total quality. Primary research was used to determine current quality characteristics in private enterprises.

This book is based on the premise that quality methods in private enterprise are applicable to educational organizations. This part of the book describes total quality as it is now being defined and pursued in the businesses and industries of the world, and examines the possibilities for fundamental transfers to school management.

Part One sets the stage for applying total quality principles from private enterprise to schools by describing the nature of total quality as practiced today in business and industry.

CHAPTER 1 ||||||||||||||||||||||||||||||||||||||||||||||||||||||||||||||||||||||||||||||||||||||||||||||||||||

The Meaning of Quality

OPERATIONAL DEFINITION OF QUALITY

Quality schools—what does that mean? Is it different from excellence or reform in education? Yes, because it uses a different standard of measurement.

Although this book will explain many specific standards that, holistically, will define quality schools, the first thing to understand is that quality schools are what the clients say they are.

In other words, quality schools are those schools that are meeting the needs of their clients. Needless to say, the term *quality* is ever evolving. What was quality in the past is not quality today, and what is quality today will not suffice as quality in the future. What remains constant in the definition, however, is the basic requirement of meeting the needs and thus satisfying the clients of the school. Clients of the school system are the students, the parents or guardians of the students, and the community that the school serves. In this sense, the term *community* is a very broad one that includes all interest groups of the community. As the application of this definition takes shape in the succeeding chapters, it will become obvious that the community will be determined by who is using the school system, and not totally by geography as is the case today.

What education has long needed is a tangible definition of how to measure the schools' educational program. Terminology and movements such as *excellence*, *reform*, or *improvement* have been dependent on arbitrary measures such as norm-referenced test scores, attendance percentages, dropout rates, or similar methods that are controversial. This is rightfully so because they are narrow instruments when compared to the broad scope of American educational aims. They fail to significantly measure the effects of demographic, psychological, and sociological factors that are beyond the control of the school system. However, client judgment is within the control of the school. Therefore, school quality is within the control of the school, and offers considerable promise as a management evaluation tool.

Some educational purists will scream that the general public is not capable of determining educational quality. They will claim that curriculum and instruction are professional endeavors to be performed by professional educators. Such an argument is, in the context of the current political, social, and educational realities, purely rhetorical. Education is in the public realm in both governance and funding. Everything else that the public pays for it eventually judges, and then chooses. Although curriculum and instructional processes are professional endeavors, the products that they produce are not. The public may not be qualified to judge the processes used, but they can and do dissect the product.

The basic premise of this book is that many aspects of quality as defined by the manufacturing and service industries of this society will significantly improve schools. For this to occur, some current educational paradigms must shift. These necessary paradigm shifts will be presented in Chapter 9. However, for the purpose of fulfilling this definition of quality schools, some form of parental choice must become part of the American school setting. This condition is necessary to define client satisfaction. In all candor, client satisfaction or dissatisfaction is present today. But since a large portion of the clients have difficulty in exercising options, the condition does not affect the schools enough to satisfy the definition of quality based on client satisfaction. The public has always paid the bill and bought the goods. Many could not choose where to shop. That has been the missing link in the quality chain.

THE NEED AND RATIONALE FOR A
QUALITY APPROACH TO SCHOOLS

In enterprises that depend on public support for their existence, perception is truth. In education, it is not just that the public must be supportive from a programmatic point of view, but it must also be supportive financially. Couple this fact with the demographics that show that less than 50 percent of the people in this country have children in the public schools, and you can see the need for schools to be perceived as top quality.

Unfortunately, that does not seem to be the case. In his book, *The Reckoning*, David Halberstam states that there are two real weaknesses in America's attempt to be competitive in the new economic era of international competition.[1] They are the public school system and the low literacy rate. He quotes the studies that concluded that if a foreign power had wanted to undermine the United States of America, it would have given it the public school system it already has. This is a perception: perhaps true, perhaps not. The significant point is that it represents a point of view shared by many groups in our society, both private and public. The public schools' approach to improvement must be based on the eradication of this perception. This nation, especially in its government and private business establishment, perceives quality as a necessity for the continued prosperity of this nation. This nation is in a new world market that is making new demands on the quality of its efforts. Education is a vital cog in this effort. The new economic world order of increased competition has naturally increased the accountability demands on schools. This accountability is taking shape in the form of technical improvements, parental choice, and other reforms that have, as a basic premise, improved quality. So the pertinent question is, what kind of quality, or quality in what form?

WHY LOOK AT QUALITY (CONTROL, ASSURANCE, SYSTEMS) IN THE MANUFACTURING AND SERVICE INDUSTRIES?

The history of the quality movement has been centered in the manufacturing and service industries; specifically, the private sector. To attempt to infuse the principles of quality without examining the concept in its historical perspective is to ignore decades of development information. So the pertinent question is not where education should go to learn about quality, but how? Specifically, education needs to distinguish those quality practices in the manufacturing and service industries that can be adapted to education, and those that cannot. Then education must devise ways to implement the practices that apply.

[1]Halberstam, D. 1986. *The Reckoning*. New York, NY: Avon Books, p. 746.

The timing is right for this process to take place. Due to the new world economic order, characterized by intense international competition in both manufacturing and service, American industry is very interested in its educational system. Industries need an effective educational base in order to compete. Specifically, they need a new type of education, one based on improved technological skills. Most important of all, they are ready, mainly for the sake of survival, to increase their support, financial and otherwise, for public education.

This renewed interest in education centers on the premise that education needs to change to meet the employment needs of the country. These needs have undergone drastic changes in recent years. During the heyday of American industry, 1946 to 1964, emphasis was on productivity, oftentimes at the expense of quality. The educational prerequisites for this assembly line era were far less in terms of academic and technical skills. With the rest of the industrial world still devastated or severely damaged from World War Two, America mistook its industrial dominance for quality superiority. Thus, they ignored long-term thinking and concentrated on immediate profits. Now we are living with the reckoning that always accompanies short-term thinking.

Since industries need to change for their own survival, they will demand that education change to meet their emerging needs. The private business establishment also has the political clout to bring about educational change. This process has already begun. Evidence of this is that they have persuaded the government at both the state and national levels to make education a top political and economic issue.

However, even if the self-serving motives just discussed were not present, education would be well served to look to industry for quality ideas and concepts. The educational establishment has become too insular. It needs to look externally for improvement ideas. Up until now, education has been asked to reform and improve its quality by external forces—parents, communities, industry, government, etc. However, although the demand is external, the means to achieve the improvement has been left to the educators. Our reaction to external demands for improvement has only resulted in more of the same, albeit in greater quantities. The only consistent effort we have made is to increase the cost. But we have been unable to show increased quality as a result of this increased cost.

Quite to the contrary, industry today is tuned into the notion of better results with the same or fewer resources. The whole society feels that we must do more with less. Education is not going to get more resources; in fact, fewer resources is a more likely reality for public education. We must adopt this mindset. Industry is ahead of us in this process. They have been working on being "leaner and meaner" for a decade or more. Also, industry has a long history of having to survive in a world of competition for customers and clients. Education is about to enter that era, which will be a new world for us. Industries know more about it than we do, and in the end, we must depend upon them for our existence, both financial and philosophical. This support is more likely if they know we are willing to join the "real world." Since education is going to become less and less institutional and move more and more into collaborative partnerships with the private sector, a quality movement will be an asset in this transition.

Incidentally, the notion of education using the private industrial complex as a role model is not new. The way schools construct facilities, organize students, implement personnel policies, including collective bargaining, and almost all other institutionalized concepts that have permeated education were borrowed from industry. Not all of their models have been good ones. The best example is collective bargaining. Too many of the concepts involved in collective bargaining were not transferable from the industrial to the educational spheres. Despite this, we bought the whole concept, lock, stock, and barrel. Education cannot buy the whole concept of quality from industry without some rejection and much alteration. But after these nontransferable areas are discarded, what remains holds tremendous promise for education. That is what this book is going to do in the remaining chapters — sifting the wheat from the chaff, and harvesting the wheat. And, most important, showing why and how it can be done.

Brief Modern History of Quality Control

Quality control has been with us since the first artisan in the one-person shop turned out a product.[2] The artisan performed all tasks, including the quality control tasks. However, when industry grew to the extent that multi-artisan shops became the norm, the master, who headed the shop, sometimes delegated quality control tasks to an assistant, who acted as an inspector of finished products. Following the Industrial Revolution, large factories became the dominant productive unit. Full-time inspectors, responsible to production foremen, performed the quality control tasks.

The next breakthrough in industrial production came with the initiation of Taylor's system of "scientific management," which separated planning from execution.[3] Taylor's methodology placed great stress on production. Quality was further jeopardized by placing quality control inspectors under production foremen. This weakness was emphasized in World War One, when American industry produced large quantities of war materials that were of very poor quality.

Prior to the 1940s there had been considerable discussion on evolving means of preventing defects from happening in the first place. These early steps toward prevention were accelerated during the 1940s by the quality control problems associated with World War Two and by the rise of the movement known as statistical quality control. It has long been said that war makes strange bedfellows. World War Two

[2]A brief, modern history of quality control will satisfy the needs of this book. For the reader who would like a detailed look at the history of quality control from ancient times until the present, I recommend: Banks, J. 1989. *Principles of Quality Control.* New York, NY: John Wiley & Sons, pp. 3–26. This work, in addition to being a thorough narrative on the subject, includes a "quality time line" which shows, in graphic form, the quality developments of each historical era.

[3]Wheeler, D. J. 1990. "Disabling and Enabling Management," *Fourth International Deming User's Group Conference, Cincinnati, OH, August 20–21, 1990,* p. 3.

became a bedfellow to quality control. American industry had trouble changing over from peacetime products to war machinery and equipment. During the war, considerable research was carried out, mostly related to probability theory in sampling and theory in process control. It was during this time that quality control took on the beginnings of "professionalism," and began to make extensive use of statistical methods. Following World War Two, American industry had the same problem in converting back to peacetime enterprises. Continued emphasis on defect prevention was the dominant thrust. Postwar quality control was based on planning and analysis. These two processes have remained as the foundation of modern day quality control.

However, the quality control theory of today has an international flavor. At the close of World War Two, both Europe and Asia were devastated by the results of the war. Only America, among the industrial powers of the world, was left intact. As a result, American industry dominated the late 1940s and 1950s in world production, and the United States mistook this production and market dominance for quality. In the meantime, the Japanese, under the tutelage of an American, W. Edwards Deming, gave a new meaning to the words *quality* and *quality control*. Once their economy had recovered from the war destruction, they, along with other recovering nations, began to challenge America's dominance. Incidentally, American industry had ignored Deming's teachings and continued to do so until the 1980s. He is today, of course, one of the leading authors and consultants on management in all the world, including his home country.

One other significant quality control trend has occurred in the 1980s and is gaining momentum in the 1990s. Once again led by the writings of Deming, a base of knowledge and theory on the quality control of service industries (like education) and the public sector of American enterprise (like education) has appeared. Significant educational writers like Glaser, Goodlad, and McNeil have helped to give the literature more substance and definition.

APPLYING QUALITY CONTROL TO SERVICE ORGANIZATIONS AND INSTITUTIONS

According to Deming,[4] a system of quality improvement is helpful to anyone who turns out a product or is engaged in service, or in research,

[4]Deming, W. E. 1991. *Out of the Crisis*. Cambridge, MA: Massachusetts Institute of Technology, Center for Advanced Engineering Study, p. 183.

and wishes to improve the output of the organization. Service needs improving as much as manufacturing does. The fact that the latest census shows that 75 out of 100 people in the United States are employed by service organizations illustrates the importance of quality service.

Most service organizations have the following characteristics:[5]

(1) Direct transactions with masses of people

(2) Large volumes of transactions

(3) Large volumes of paperwork

(4) Large amounts of processing

(5) An extremely large number of ways to make errors

(6) Handling and rehandling of huge numbers of small items in communication

One of the significant aspects of these characteristics is that mistakes are costly, not so much in terms of money as in terms of the process and the product. Also, the further the mistake goes without correction, the greater the cost to the persons involved. This is especially true in education, where the accumulation of mistakes creates seemingly insurmountable problems.

There are some obvious differences between service and manufacturing, among them the fact that service institutions have a more captive market and do not, as a rule, generate new products or materials.

However, there is one difference that is very significant to the application of quality control principles to service organizations and institutions. In organizations where the worker is producing a product, he/she not only has a job, but is doing his/her part to make something that somebody will see, feel, and use in some way. Also, he/she knows what the desired quality is and how to perform the operation to contribute to the final product quality.

In service organizations/institutions, too many workers only see that they have a job. They can't visualize the final product, nor can they see what they contributed to the quality of the final product or service. Therefore, quality is often missing.

APPLICATION OF TOTAL QUALITY TO EDUCATIONAL INSTITUTIONS

Total quality is a management tool. There seems to be consensus

[5]Ibid., p. 189.

among the American society that education is in need of new ways of management that focus on quality. Goodlad states it this way:[6]

> There is no shortage of good ideas about ways to solve the problems of our schools. Good as they are, however, these ideas have not taken hold and will not take hold, because of the way our schools are managed. Before anything else will work, we need to replace the way we manage now with a new method of management that focuses on quality.

The industrial analogy that compares workers and managers to students and teachers is accurate and appropriate. In schools, students are the workers and the products. Teachers and administrators are the managers. The hierarchy looks like this.

(1) *Students* are the workers and the products. The difference between success and failure of the school depends on the quality of their work.

(2) *Teachers* are the first-level managers. Therefore, the teacher will be the leader of the class, emphasizing quality through noncoercive management featuring student as worker and teacher as coach, provoking the students to learn how to learn and thus to teach themselves.

(3) *Administrators* are middle and upper level management. The productivity of any school depends mostly on the skills of those who directly manage the workers, i.e., the teachers. According to Deming, their success in turn depends on how well they are managed by the administration above them. Therefore, any attempts at educational quality are best centered around organizational improvement efforts.

(4) *The Board of Education* is the board of directors, thus responsible directly to the clients, and board members are the overseers of the administration.

CURRENT STATUS OF QUALITY SYSTEMS IN INDUSTRY

To understand the current status of the quality movement in American industry, one must revisit the end of World War Two. Industrial Europe had been devastated by Allied and Axis bombs. Japan's indus-

[6]Glasser, W. 1990. "The Quality School," *Phi Delta Kappan* (February):425.

trial might lay in ruins. Therefore, in the world's industrial market, the United States emerged as the only industrial power whose manufacturing capacity was intact.

What followed, up until around 1964, was a giant American industrial juggernaut supplying manufactured goods for the world without significant competition. The United States mistook this dominance for quality, and the country turned away from quality experts such as Deming. There was no time for long-term thinking about quality, in an atmosphere where quarterly profits drove American companies. Executives lived and died by the numbers. Growth was the measurement for quality. American industry was growing, it was reasoned, so therefore, it must be producing quality products.

Simultaneous to the postwar growth of American industry, a trend was occurring that had a profound effect on the quality of American products and services. The long-term effects of this event on quality would not show up until the reappearance of international competition, especially Japan, in the 1960s. This event was the rise of union power, and the results of this increased power, that is: higher wages, increased health benefits, and an increase in worker independence.

This power was brought about through the collective bargaining process, which was built on an adversarial relationship and the pursuit of self-interests. In companies where the extreme occurred, workers perceived themselves as employees of the union, not of the company. In times of union/management controversy or worker unrest, the sabotage of quality by workers was not uncommon.

The state of affairs of industrial unions during the 1960s has special relevance to education. When schools adopted professional negotiations with teachers and noncertificated personnel in the 1960s and 1970s, they adopted the industrial model for master contract language and bargaining procedures. Currently, industry is attempting to improve its quality by altering both union/management relations and the bargaining process.

Basically, the current quality effort in American industry is an attempt to catch up with foreign competition in quality, particularly Japan, by undoing the results of these two historical trends. The foreign competition doesn't have either of these situations (apathy toward quality or labor problems) to overcome.

The current state of affairs in industrial quality is well illustrated by the changing terminology. In the 1970s, the term *quality control* gave way to the new term, *quality assurance*. Today, the terms indicate that control and assurance, which suggest some form of inspection, have been replaced by emphasis on the total involvement of personnel and operations. Examples of this are *total quality management*, *total quality*, and *total quality system*.

Control is not the essential element in today's quality efforts. The essential element is a total company response, both by management and workers, to the quality concept.

One way to show the difference between *quality control*, the recent past, and *total quality*, the present, is to show the change from the pipeline to the cyclical models of management.

THE PIPELINE MODEL

In 1938 Walter Shewhart presented the notion that there were three steps in the quality control process: the specification of what is wanted, the production of things to satisfy the specification, and the inspection of the things produced to see if they satisfy the specification.[7] Under the old notion of production, these three steps were thought of as independent of each other. One person could specify what he/she wanted, someone else could take this specification as a guide and make the thing, and an inspector could measure the thing to see if it met specifications. Figure 2.1 pictures these three steps sequentially.

This worldview grew out of the manufacturing experiences of the 1800s, and is still seen in operation today. The lack of feedback from steps two and three to step one results in a specification-driven ap-

Figure 2.1 The old view (pipeline model).

[7]Shewhart, W. A. 1986. *Statistical Method from the Viewpoint of Quality Control.* Washington, DC: Graduate Department of Agriculture, p. 6 (originally published in 1939 by Dover).

proach to production. The purpose of inspection is to sort the good stuff from the bad, and efforts come to be focused on improving the sorting process. When methods of sorting to check specifications became cheap and efficient, the emphasis quickly shifted to meeting the production schedule, and any thoughts about changing the process were simply nonexistent so long as production schedules were being met. While this approach will produce parts that fit together (most of the time) and products that will function (more or less), it leaves behind a costly pile of scrap.

With the pipeline model, the emphasis is upon meeting the specifications by sorting the conforming components from the nonconforming ones. Naturally, given the amount of time and energy needed for the inspection operation, there is little time left for thinking about the process at all, much less for thinking about how to improve the process. Scrap and rework came to be thought of as inevitable, and budgets were written which incorporated costs for these errors. The higher the product quality, the higher the scrap and rework costs. While Shewhart called this the old view of production in 1938, it is unfortunately still in use today.

This pipeline view has been adapted to many new situations that characterize today's industries. For example, product development is still viewed as a pipeline. Basic research is done by some elite group. They experiment, discover some basic relationships, and then pass the project on to a development group. The development group makes prototypes and tinkers with the project design. When the product design is nearly finalized, the process engineering group is asked to develop a manufacturing process.

Notice the linear nature of this process. Once each group had finished with its part of the project, it moved on to other things. Of course, in reality, each group is working on several projects, and the confusion that exists slows down each of the projects. If one group has failed to do all that it needed to do, it is left for the next group to take up the slack. Of course they never do, and it is finally dumped in the lap of manufacturing, which tries to compensate by taking their best shot at making the product despite the gaps in knowledge, understanding, and development.

If the product is inferior, or doesn't work as intended, then the company vows that it will do better next time. There is no thought to fixing the current product unless it absolutely has to be done.

FREDERICK TAYLOR AND "SCIENTIFIC MANAGEMENT"

Management philosophy can be defined as the ways in which management exerts control. When a major change in manufacturing takes place, management philosophies will eventually be adjusted to accommodate the change. One of the most pronounced changes in manufacturing was the assembly line, which some have called the Second Wave of the Industrial Revolution. One of the first efforts to codify the new management philosophy that led to the assembly line was Frederick Taylor's book, entitled *Principles of Scientific Management.* Among the philosophical presuppositions used by Taylor was the pipeline view of production. Since everything was directed down toward manufacturing, the focus was on how to increase efficiency and productivity by defining systems and operations more rigorously. The major thrust of Taylor's management philosophy has been summarized by a set of axioms, first suggested by Perry Gluckman.[8]

(1) Control of a business is established by staffing positions of responsibility and authority with professional managers trained in the theory of "scientific management."

(2) Improvements are due to increasing the division of work and increasing the concurrency of work.

(3) Systems are developed to perform repetitive tasks.

(4) The information will be available to create an optimum system; an optimum system can be created by the proper formulation of the objectives of the system and the evaluation of the alternatives to meet these objectives.

(5) Once a system has been properly defined and installed, any failure to meet stated objectives must come from outside the system.

(6) The status of the system is continuously monitored for deviation from system objectives to see if improper worker selection, poor motivation, inadequate training, or weak supervision are the causes of missed objectives.

What are the consequences of these axioms? Well, first of all, management effectiveness is perceived as coming from the power of posi-

[8]Wheeler, D. J. 1990. "Disabling and Enabling Management," *Fourth International Deming User's Group Conference, Cincinnati, OH, August 20–21, 1990*, p. 3.

tion. Authority is the key to effectiveness. With authority, one can attempt to force others to do that which one wants them to do. Given a big enough carrot and stick, a manager can supposedly get almost anything done. This myth is verbalized every day in the business sections of the newspapers when new CEOs are described as tough, lean, and effective at cutting costs. When was the last time you heard or read of a CEO described as knowledgeable about the product, innovative, able to inspire others, and able to define and produce desirable products?

Secondly, management is seen to be an exercise in setting goals. Management by objectives, pay for performance, merit pay, work standards, incentive pay, management by results, management by the imposition of results, and all of their debilitating cousins are the logical consequence of this set of axioms. Also, these axioms suggest that goals are just specifications on performance, and are a primary tool for shifting blame.

Thirdly, the development of systems is the primary function of management and technical personnel. Systems must be created, developed, and implemented in order to organize the work in an effective manner. The workers are merely there to run the system.

Fourthly, with this emphasis upon systems, it is necessary to obtain good business forecasts in order to develop optimum systems. Elaborate forecasting and expensive strategic planning are seen as the key to assuring that the systems will be effective in the future. Once the system is in place, it will be expensive to modify or replace it, since all the work in the pipeline takes a considerable amount of time and effort. Therefore, even more work is required to ensure that the system is a good one.

Finally, the inevitable consequence of Taylor's management philosophy is the practice of scapegoating. When the system does not perform as intended (and systems seldom do), it is natural to search for who was to blame. Remember, the system is optimal. The company spent millions to make it optimal. Therefore, since the fault cannot be in the system, it must be in personnel, or else it is the fault of suppliers or clients.

So, the Taylor philosophy of management places people at the end of the pipeline, where they receive an operating system over which they have no control, and which then holds them accountable for the results of that system. This system is bureaucratic, authoritarian, centrally planned, rigid, and inflexible. The greatest experiments with the use of this philosophy have recently ended. They were the governments of Eastern Europe, including the Soviet Union.

THE CYCLIC MODEL

At the same time that Walter Shewhart described the pipeline model, he also gave the cyclic model,[9] shown in Figure 2.2. This notion of specification, production, and inspection as an ongoing cycle has profoundly different consequences than the pipeline model.

In terms of the control of quality, the cyclic model shows that the three steps are not independent. They are interlocking. In order to set meaningful specifications, one must have some knowledge of production capabilities, and these capabilities must be determined by inspection. One cannot know exactly what to inspect unless one has some concept of just what characteristics are important. Thus, the three steps are interlocked. This cycle is more appropriate for the real world than the pipeline model.

Shewhart adapted the cyclic model from the steps of the scientific method — formulate a hypothesis, perform an experiment, and analyze

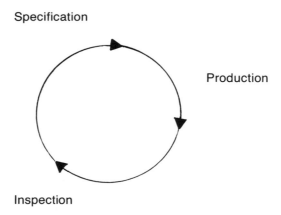

Figure 2.2 The cyclic model.

[9]Shewhart, W. A. 1986. *Statistical Method from the Viewpoint of Quality Control.* Washington, DC: Graduate Department of Agriculture, p. 6 (originally published in 1939 by Dover).

the results of that experiment. In his own words, "These three steps form a dynamic scientific process of acquiring knowledge." This is why the cyclic model is being used so much in contemporary quality systems, and is at the very heart of current theory of management. The best example of the current management thinking is that of Deming, whose theory of management is characterized by the following axioms.[10]

(1) Control of a business is established by leadership and cooperation.

(2) Improvements are due to increasing the division of work, information, and creativity, and to increasing the concurrency of work.

(3) Systems are developed to perform repetitive tasks.

(4) No system is ever truly an optimum system; every system must be analyzed to understand the natural behavior of the system and the variation of the system.

(5) Inconsistencies and contradictions that become apparent upon analysis of the system may be used to detect and isolate the built-in flaws in the system.

(6) A secure environment is created so that everyone can apply the first five axioms without fear. Offer support, reassurance, and appreciation.

The consequences of these axioms are quite different than the ones resulting from the pipeline model. Since intrinsic motivation is much more powerful than extrinsic motivation, managers who exercise leadership will always be more effective than those who depend upon extrinsic motivation. Carrots and sticks just cannot compete with intrinsic motivation. This is why some knowledge of psychology is an integral part of Deming's system of profound knowledge.

The setting of goals and targets is a symptom of management trying to duck its leadership role. When one person sets a goal, he/she shifts the responsibility onto someone else. Goals distort the system, and can ultimately wreck the organization, but they get the monkey off the back of the one who set the goal.

Flexible systems, which are formulated in part by those who use them, can respond to changes in the environment when they occur.

[10]Wheeler, D. J. 1990. "Disabling and Enabling Management," *Fourth International Deming User's Group Conference, Cincinnati, OH, August 20–21, 1990*, pp. 6–8.

There is less emphasis on forecasting, and greater emphasis on making the system work. This naturally leads to the concept of *continual improvement*.

As long as a system is viewed as being optimal, there is no freedom to tinker with the system. Continual improvement will not be an option. However, when people are no longer trapped within a system imposed from above, they can begin to work to make needed changes in the system. Barriers to quality and productivity can be removed. Problems can be addressed immediately, not at the end of the production. And the worker can begin to take pride in his/her job, because now the worker can contribute to that job.

Two examples of the cyclic model in the works of Dr. Edwards Deming are the PDSA cycle and the Production Viewed as a System diagram (see Figure 2.3).

Dr. Deming's PDSA cycle divides Shewhart's inspection step into two steps (study-act), but otherwise the elements are recognizable. In terms of production, this cycle could be expressed as:

- Plan incremental changes in product or process.
- Make these changes.
- Study the effects of these changes.
- Act appropriately based on what has been discovered from the changes.

These two versions of the cyclic model address both the internal feedback for product and process improvement, and the external feedback for adapting to, and even anticipating, market trends. When combined, the benefit and power of these cyclic models is apparent.

These cyclic models match the way we learn about the world around us. When they are made a part of the natural way of operation, they facilitate incremental improvements. Since incremental improvements are easier to implement than major breakthroughs, the company becomes more responsive, more flexible. New technologies are more easily adopted, and production problems can be fixed in successive cycles as the products and processes are continually refined. When applied to product development, the cyclic model will often shorten the lead times by creating a better base of knowledge concerning the capabilities and limitations of production processes. With shorter cycles the company will experience a quicker return on investment, and a faster response to a changing market.

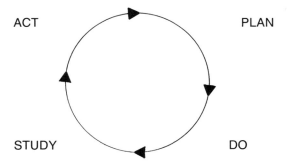

The Production Viewed as a System diagram shows how a manufacturing operation can continue to be competitive in an evolving marketplace.

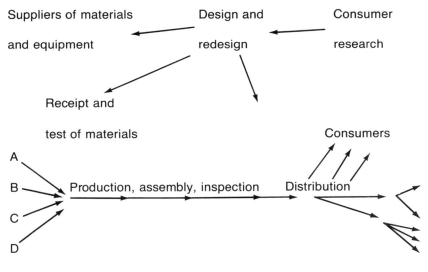

***Figure* 2.3** *Production Viewed as a System (adapted from Deming, W. Edwards. 1991.* Out of the Crisis. *Cambridge, MA: MIT Press).*

Finally, the use of cyclic models will lead to a better utilization of the people in an organization, since virtually all levels of personnel will be involved in the cyclic improvements.

To help people to do their jobs to the best of their ability, so that they can go home each day satisfied that they have made a contribution, is the essence of this approach to quality management.

Characteristics of Quality Systems in Private Enterprise

Quality systems in industry have provided some amazing successes for American business. Some of these principles are applicable to education, and some are not. The purpose of this chapter is to present those principles that are applicable to schools and which will result in the improvement of education.

The format of this chapter is as follows. First, the research base will be presented. Then the characteristics of industrial/commercial quality systems identified by the primary research and supported by the secondary research will be presented and described. In Part Two of the book (Chapters 4 through 9) a practical discussion of how the quality principles can be adapted to education will be presented.

THE RESEARCH DESIGN

This book was produced from a combination of primary and secondary research. The primary component consisted of direct contact with eight private companies through interviews with high-level quality officers, and observation of the quality systems of the eight companies in operation. The secondary component consisted of readings, videotapes, and seminars centering around the concept of quality. The primary research effort occurred during 1990, 1991, and 1992. The secondary inquiry has been ongoing for the last five years.

Primary Research

The Companies

The following eight companies were the subjects in the primary research:

(1) American Telephone and Telegraph (AT&T)
(2) Cincinnati Gas and Electric
(3) Cincinnati Milicron
(4) Ford Motor Company (Batavia, Ohio plant)
(5) General Electric
(6) Kroger food chain
(7) Procter and Gamble
(8) Robin Color Lab

These companies represent both the manufacturing and service industries. They also vary in size, especially in the key factor of number of employees. The number of employees in the larger firms, such as General Electric, is in the thousands. Robin Color Lab, on the other hand, employs between forty and fifty people.

Within these eight companies, the following manufacturing or service processes are found — communications (AT&T), public utilities (Cincinnati Gas and Electric), machine tool, plastics manufacturing (Cincinnati Milicron), automobile transmission manufacturing (Ford Motor Company), jet engine manufacturing (General Electric), food retailing (Kroger), diverse product manufacturing (Procter and Gamble), and industrial printing (Robin Color Lab).

The actual dates and places of the initial interviews, as well as the names of the persons interviewed, are listed in the Appendix.

Observations of the Quality Efforts in the Eight Companies

This phase of the research consisted of extensive examination of quality plans and processes, training schemes, agendas and evaluations, actual participation in the training programs, participating in the planning and implementation of training/retraining in total quality concepts, conducting and facilitating training sessions in total quality concepts, observing manufacturing and services in operation, and talking informally with workers and management at all levels.

Secondary Research

The secondary research effort was centered on the quality literature and research aimed at the business and industrial world. Many of the sources, such as Deming's *Out of the Crisis*, contained references and applications to the service industries, to which education was assigned. Of course, if I found articles in educational periodicals that were devoted to the concept of quality, such as Glasser's "The Quality School, What Motivates the Ants?" in the February, 1990 *Kappan*, I read them with great interest and used them when appropriate. However, the majority of my secondary research, in keeping with the theme of the book, was devoted to quality literature and research in the private sector.

I maintained this posture in my pursuit of the media, especially the vast resources available in videotapes. Chief among these were the futurist tapes of Joel Barker and the vast Deming library.

Perhaps the most valuable aspect of the secondary research effort was my attendance at workshops and seminars that were primarily designed for upper and middle management of business and industry on the concept of quality, primarily the specific concept of total quality management. I am happy to report that recently I have not always been the only educator present.

Strengths of the Research Design

It Bridges the Philosophical and Intellectual Gap between the Private Sector and Public Education

Many prominent Americans, in both the private and public sector, have been calling for the application of business principles to many aspects of education, including curriculum, instruction, and management. However, many of these exhortations consist more of rhetoric than of specific and accurate suggestions. They are based on frustration with the educational establishment, which is not meeting their needs with regard to skill preparation.

These private enterprise people believe that school organizations are just like their own organizations. Therefore, their business practices would work for schools. What they haven't done is to study school organizational structure and culture. There are differences in both culture and structure that need to be considered when applying business practices and principles to schools. Until those differences are studied, the potential to use business practices in schools cannot be achieved.

On the other hand, too many members of the educational establishment have been skeptical of even considering the notion that there may be many aspects of business and industrial operations that could be beneficial to schools. The simple fact that schools do not manufacture anything, or that they are not in business to turn a profit is (for them) significant evidence that such things as quality control won't work in schools.

This is rhetorical also, at least at this stage of the discussion. And it will continue to be until educators study the methods of business and industry to the point that any rejection or acceptance is based on un-biased research and study.

This research base is designed to avoid both these positions. The in-dustrial quality methods have been carefully observed and analyzed. Also, no preconceived rejection of any of their practices is present. However, each industrial practice is discussed, with a thorough ex-amination of the obstacles and constraints that the educational culture and structure present.

In other words, the research has eliminated the fence between the two enterprises. Instead of each standing on their side of the fence and shouting suggestions across the fence, the research has visited both backyards and is now attempting to see if the fence can be taken out so that both neighbors can work together to sow some new grass in the old fence row.

Interview Technique

Successful businesses and industries are not anxious to share their quality successes with competitors. Industrial security is a fact. How-ever, this fact became a strength in my research process. By talking face to face with quality experts I was able to prove to them that my purpose was not to take advantage of them, or be a competitor, but to try to improve the way schools approach quality management. They were very anxious to see me succeed. Everyone that I interviewed is a stakeholder in the public school system.

The interview technique broadened and enriched the text. It enabled me to fully tap the knowledge base of these quality experts. It wasn't limiting, as a questionnaire sometimes can be. I let them take me to questions and discussions that I did not have the knowledge base to pursue without their lead.

Each interview asked two broad questions. These questions were the proactive part of the interview, as well as the control mechanism to keep the interviews as standard as possible. These questions were, "How does your company define quality?" and, "What does your company do to insure that the services and products that you provide meet your quality expectations?"

All other questions revolved from the response to these two questions and produced the common quality characteristics identified in this chapter. The initial interviews lasted from one and one-half hours to four hours. Follow-up interviews varied from one-half hour to two hours. Inevitably, they would explain the nature of their quality efforts, including philosophy and organization. As the discussion continued, I was able to gain a perspective of their total quality company effort. The unrestricted responses enabled me to determine the common characteristics of their quality efforts. Those common characteristics make up the volume of the text.

Noneducational Literature Base

There is no way that a book on quality could be properly researched using only the educational literature. Quality is a concept born and developed in private enterprise. Therefore, although there is no claim that it makes it a better bibliography, the noneducational leadership base of my research is different than what one would find in most educational leadership or management books. Therefore, the bibliography adds to, and does not just embellish, the literature in school management.

Weaknesses of the Research Design

The interviews produced diverse and varied information that did not lend itself to a neat statistical analysis. Also, the information generated by the interviews consisted largely of the opinions of the people being interviewed. Although I attempted to substantiate their opinions through observations and examinations of verification documents, all the weaknesses of human endeavors like interviews and observations are hereby noted and accepted.

Keep in mind that I was observing operations in which I had little or no experience. Also, the time spent observing was not sufficient to make a claim that I fully understood the operation or process. However, the time and expertise was sufficient to verify that the characteristics identified by the interviews were, in fact, the ingredients of the company's quality efforts. To quote Kumi, "accept regular tendency which appears in a large number of observational results as reliable information."

THE SEVENTEEN QUALITY CHARACTERISTICS

The intent of the research was to determine the nature of quality efforts in private enterprise. Since the primary method chosen was interviews and observation, supplemented by secondary research, my personal background was vital to the success of the venture. Having worked in private industry in both manufacturing and quality control makes the design more credible.

I consider this effort an initial one in a research area that will continue to grow and become more refined. My biggest hope is that this book will stimulate people in both education and industry to study each other more closely, for the purpose of helping and understanding one another better. I found that industrial executives feel that they are in the midst of a transformation that is not complete. This research is a description of where they are, and where they are attempting to go with quality efforts.

To be listed as a characteristic of quality efforts in private enterprise, the following criteria had to be met. First of all, all eight companies had to identify it in the interview process as a component of their quality effort. Secondly, the component had to be verified either through documentation or observation. And last of all, the component had to be supported in the secondary research as a major component of contemporary quality efforts.

Based on these three criteria, the following seventeen common characteristics of quality efforts were identified:

(1) A continuous improvement standard
(2) The use of consumer research
(3) The external quality concept
(4) Quality function deployment
(5) Statistical process control
(6) The internal quality concept
(7) The use of human sensors
(8) Quality teams

(9) Flattening the hierarchy

(10) Natural work groups

(11) Empowerment

(12) Abandonment

(13) Reduction in inspection

(14) Change in management philosophy

(15) The 85/15 rule

(16) Quality as a people issue

(17) Employee suggestion program

We will now examine each of these quality characteristics in greater detail.

Quality Characteristic 1—A Continuous Improvement Standard

The old concept of quality control was built on preestablished standards, specifications, units of measure, sensors, and tolerances. The whole operation was considered successful if the operator managed to stay within the tolerances. Remember that tolerance is the maximum amount of error allowed by inspection. If for example a casting was to be ground to a diameter of 12 inches, the tolerance could be plus or minus 1/32 of an inch. That means that if the casting was ground to a diameter of 12 and 1/32 inches, it would be within tolerance and would thus pass inspection. If another casting was ground to a diameter of 11 and 31/32 inches, it would also pass inspection.

The problems resulting from "tolerance" thinking are obvious. If all the castings were ground to exactly 12 inches, they would be of better quality than castings that were off by plus or minus 1/32 of an inch. If more than one of these castings went into the same product, and they were all off the maximum tolerance, the machine would be difficult to assemble and would not be a well-functioning machine. If this machine was made up of one hundred parts, all of which were produced at the maximum tolerance, you can imagine what would happen. You already know what happens. You have been using these products all your life. Now you know why you couldn't get that last self-assembled house tool to go together without the use of a persuader (a hammer and all your strength).

Today, the idea of staying within set tolerances as the quality goal has been replaced by continuous improvement based on control limits. To illustrate how this new concept works, take a look at Figure 3.1.

The letters UCL mean upper control limits. The letters LCL mean lower control limits. Figure 3.1(a) represents the performance level over a significant time. Notice on the line graph of Figure 3.1(a) that the new castings being machined reached the upper and lower tolerance level on one occasion each. However, on the vast majority of occasions, the operation was performed at a much smaller tolerance. This would seem to indicate that the tolerance could be lowered without jeopardizing production. Needless to say, quality would be improved.

Therefore, based on the proven performance, new upper and lower control limits are established which reflect the improved performance. Figure 3.1(b) shows the new upper and lower control limits or tolerances. At the conclusion of operations shown in Figure 3.1(c), the limits could be reduced again. This continual process of lowering the control limits (amount of error acceptable based on performance data) is the concept of continuous improvement.

Under the old systems of quality control, tolerances would remain in place for long periods of time. They were only changed when a competitor did a better job and began stealing the company's customers or clients. Under the new concept of continuous improvement, you not only try to meet customers' needs (which the upper and lower control limits were doing), but to exceed them through continuous improvement, and to go beyond the customers' expectations and show them the way to self-improvement. That is the way companies are trying to keep customers today. Their theory is "If you don't do it, someone else will."

Theoretically, the upper and lower limits will continue to be reduced until the tolerance is eliminated. (In this case all the castings would have identical diameters—12 inches.)

The key to the whole concept of continuous improvement is that standards and tolerances are not static. Instead, standards are based on updated performance data.

It is only through the improvement of the process that continuous improvement can take place. Therefore, the continuous improvement thrust has shifted emphasis from product inspection to the study of process. The only way to achieve continuous improvement is through changing the system.

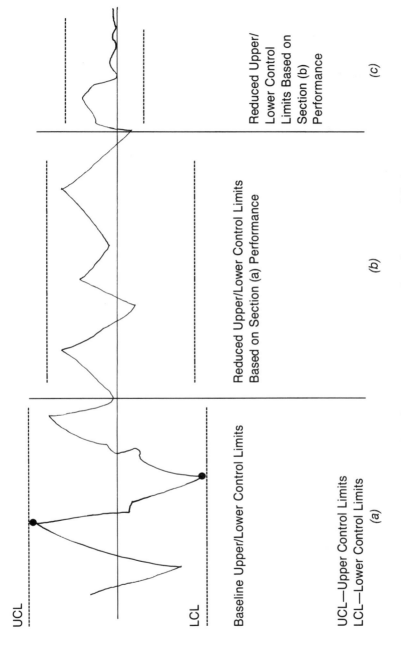

Figure 3.1 Continuous improvement based on control limits.

UCL

LCL

Baseline Upper/Lower Control Limits

(a)

UCL—Upper Control Limits
LCL—Lower Control Limits

Reduced Upper/Lower Control Limits
Based on Section (a) Performance

(b)

Reduced Upper/
Lower Control
Limits Based on
Section (b)
Performance

(c)

Quality Characteristic 2—The Use of Consumer Research

In order to use consumer research, quality characteristics must be identified. For example, The Kroger Company bases its consumer research on eleven characteristics. Among them are price competitiveness, quantity and quality of sales, quality of advertising, courtesy of employees, speed of checkout, facility conditions such as the cleanliness of the store, and how well the shelves are stocked. All research efforts are then directed toward assessing public beliefs about the company's quality based on these characteristics.

Research results are used for the following purposes.

(1) They confirm the company's belief in what is good about the company (positive reinforcement).

(2) They encourage management to combine research with other information in making decisions. Sometimes research will indicate the need for a major overhaul in some operation of the company, but such an overhaul is too expensive to be feasible. Therefore, it is accurate to say that consumer research plus common sense is used in making decisions.

(3) Results of tracking research are used continuously to compile statistics over a period of time to verify information such as trends or facts.

(4) They identify problems and successes within the company that no other method or strategy is able to do.

(5) They motivate and reward employees.

The role of the research departments in industry are (1) pulling the research together in a presentable and readable form, (2) interpreting the results, (3) presenting the results to company personnel throughout the company, both management and labor, and (4) constantly monitoring trends.[11]

The research methods are key to the success or failure of the effort. Almost all of the consumer research is conducted by phone. Calls are made between 5 and 9 P.M. on weekdays, and from 10 A.M. till 7 P.M. on Saturday. These times and the phone method are both used because they have been found to be the most effective methods of reaching the

[11]Wolfran, K. Director, Consumer Research, The Kroger Company, Cincinnati, Ohio. Interview, 7 Jan., 1991.

primary client, and the only way to consistently get a random sample. A random sample is necessary for accurate consumer research. Interviews last ten to twelve minutes on the average. Private companies often contract with marketing specialist firms to do the calling. This is done when the company does not have the permanent personnel to conduct the calls. Also, it is often used by companies whose consumer research is only done periodically, and not on an ongoing basis.

Interestingly, the industries interviewed did not tend to compare results from one geographical area to another. They explained that the demographics were too different. Therefore, their consumer research efforts were regional, and the results applied regionally. However, they did make regional results available on a national scale as a way for the entire company to possibly predict future trends.

As with research in any field, consumer research oftentimes has a lag between the research itself and sales or other trends, sometimes positive and sometimes negative. Said another way, the research may indicate a downward trend while current results may be upward in nature, or vice versa. Actual consumer practices tend to change more slowly than the research results. These facts tend to make research a predictor in many cases. However, they also make the results hard to sell to reluctant management.

In summary, then, consumer research, in the opinion of private enterprise, identifies problems and successes within the company that no other method or strategy is able to do. Because of this belief, consumer research drives the decision making of many companies, especially in the retail business.

The consumer research people studied in this research consistently suggested that many of the people in middle management felt that the companies were driven too much by consumer research. Therefore, to get the company to use consumer research in making decisions, a champion for "the cause" is needed. In Kroger's case, the chairman of the board said, "we will use consumer research." Bonuses and raises were tied to the use of the research. However, due to the success of Kroger's consumer research efforts over the past seventeen years, such motivators are no longer necessary.

One last note about consumer research as practiced in the private sector—customers are asked to compare the company's products and services with those of the competitors in that geographical area. So you see, the consumer research is based on a competitive model. The information desired is twofold. First, are our products and services of good quality? And second, how do we compare with our chief competitors?

Quality Characteristic 3—The External Quality Concept

External quality in the private sector involves working with vendors and suppliers. As per Deming's point, the trend is to attempt to create long-term, trusting relationships with a smaller number of vendors. Therefore, industry has become more interested in a long-term relationship with fewer vendors, emphasizing quality over a low price tag. This is another attempt at getting away from inspection as a means of controlling quality. Companies now send their own employees out to the vendors during the manufacturing process of the vendor to insure specifications and quality adherence. This integrated approach is also used by companies when they bring representatives of the vendor to their workplace so they can see firsthand what their product is expected to do. They continuously "walk a mile in each others' shoes."

Companies (i.e., General Electric)[12] continuously train their vendors in their expectations. They don't expect them to have this expertise, so they provide it themselves. That is another reason they are interested in long-term relationships. They have invested heavily in the vendor's training and future.

In summary, to insure external quality, the industrial sector must (1) bring the vendors into their workplace to illustrate their expectation, (2) observe the vendors' manufacturing processes to insure quality during the process, (3) eliminate inspection of incoming vendor parts or products, (4) provide training to the vendors on their quality expectation, (5) "walk a mile in each others' shoes," (6) cut down the number of vendors, (7) develop long-term relationships with vendors based on quality service and products, not the price tag alone.

Quality Characteristic 4—Quality Function Deployment

Industry defines quality function deployment as the shifting of power from the manufacturer to the customer. As was pointed out in the first chapter, the universal definition of quality by all the industries studied in this research defined quality as "what the customer says it is."

[12]Robinson, P. W. Manager, Evendale Quality Training and Support, Cincinnati, Ohio. Interview, 10 Jan., 1991.

Prior to the development of the intense national and international competition that has emerged in the last two decades for the world's goods and services, manufacturers often made decisions about their own industry that determined quality. Things went badly for them when foreign competitors, especially the Japanese, based their quality decisions on what the customer wanted.

This shifting of power from the manufacturer to the customer is accomplished through a process whereby the manufacturer sends its employees to the customer's plant or service agency to find out, first hand, what the customer does with the product that the manufacturer is going to make for them. In this way, it becomes very clear to the manufacturer exactly what the customer wants the product or service to perform.

Perhaps an actual example from the research effort will clarify what is meant by quality function deployment. One of the companies that I studied is involved in serving the public through delicatessens. Their store design experts constantly work to improve the design of their stores. These designs are drawn up by engineers for delivery to the stores.

This company also conducts extensive consumer research. I asked them what they would do if their consumer research conflicted with their design experts. In other words, what if the members of the public said that they wanted their delicatessen to look different than the design the experts had developed. The answer was quick and definitive. The delicatessen would reflect the consumer research. The customer research would drive the company. That is what is meant by quality function deployment.

Quality Characteristic 5—Statistical Process Control

This process consists of training and implementation on the following topics:

- common cause vs. special cause
- variability
- probability plotting
- variable control charts
- X and R charts
- capable process studies

The key to industry's statistical process control of quality is the differentiation between common cause and special cause. Common cause is random variation that is not controllable. Efforts to improve quality in these areas only bring frustration and diminishing returns with severe human costs. Special causes are mechanical, fatigue, or other causes that can be remedied. Therefore, they are assignable and treatable. Also, they can be accountable in nature. Needless to say, current quality efforts in industry center around special causes only.

The concepts of variability and probability are treated through the extensive use of charts, often referred to as probability plotting, variable control charts, and X or R charts. These charts, which plot performance on a day-to-day basis, are visible and thus constant reminders for both management and workers as to how they are doing with quality. Following are examples of quality charts as used by industry (see Figures 3.2–3.9).[13]

Quality Characteristic 6—The Internal Quality Concept

Internal quality in industry is best summed up in the question, "What can I do to help you do your job better?" This question is asked by the person who is performing a function (job) to the person who will perform the next function (job). Following this goal, industry has created an integrated approach to the manufacturing or service process. All workers affected by an operation learn more about what their fellow workers do, and spend time trying to figure out what each of them can do to make the others more effective. This integrated approach applies in planning as well as operations. For example, engineers do not design operations without consulting with the workers who will perform the actual work. This is sometimes referred to as concurrent engineering.

In both planning and operations, continual dialogue, instruction, and questioning take place to improve quality. No longer does industry plan on a departmental basis. The whole operation is planned in an integrated format. This concept requires more time because workers must learn other people's jobs in addition to their own. The payoff is that because they know what the other person is doing, they will be able to

---

[13]Scholtes, P. R. et al. 1989. *The Team Handbook, How to Use Teams to Improve Quality.* Madison, WI: Joiner Associates, Inc., pp. 2-36, 2-24, 2-25, 2-26, 2-32, 2-33, 2-34, 2-35, respectively.

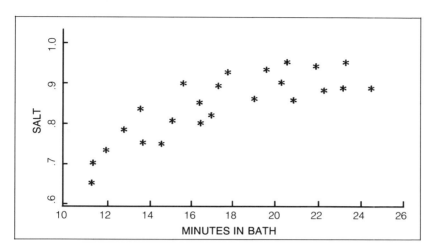

Scatter diagrams display the relationship between two process characteristics.

Whereas a dot plot allows you to look at only one process characteristic at a time, a scatter diagram lets you look at the relationship between two characteristics.

Suppose salt content of cheese is an important quality characteristic. To see what factors influence this characteristic, you measure both the salt content of a piece of cheese and the time it stayed in a salt bath of known salinity. For each piece of cheese, there are a pair of measurements: salt content and time in the bath. Instead of making two separate dot plots, you can combine the two: marking salt content along the horizontal axis (sometimes called the X axis) and time along the vertical axis (sometimes called the Y axis). You place points where the values of each pair intersect.

The shape of the resulting scatter of points tells you if the two factors are related. If they are unrelated, the points will be randomly scattered around the graph. If larger values of one occur with larger values of the other, the points will group towards a line running from lower left to upper right; if larger values of one are associated with smaller values of the other, the points will cluster on a line running from upper left to lower right.

Figure 3.2 *Scatter diagram (reprinted from* The Team Handbook*).*

Step	Rene	Jacob	Olga	Manuel
Plan the Report	Everyone's responsibility			
Organize the Report	■	○		
Write the Report	■		■	
Produce the Report		○		■

Deployment charts show both the flow of a process and which people or groups are involved at each step. The one shown here depicts how the "report preparation flowchart" described previously (pp. 2-18 and 2-19) might look as a deployment chart. The shaded boxes indicate who has primary responsibility for that step; the ovals indicate a helper or advisor.

A deployment chart combines two ideas: what happens in a process or project (the tasks accomplished) and who is responsible for each step. These charts show the major steps of a process, just as in the top level of a top-down flowchart, along with which person or group is the center of activity for that step. These charts are useful for project teams and management teams to keep track of what each person or group is supposed to do, where the people involved fit in the sequence, and how they will relate to the other players at that stage.

To construct a deployment chart, list the major steps of a project or process vertically on a page. List each of the players—individuals or groups—across the top, and draw lines to create columns under each heading. Then mark the key action at each step in the appropriate column, denoting which person or group is responsible for that step. You can even use different symbols to indicate different kinds of roles at each stage (such as "primary responsibility" or "advisor"). If you use different symbols, anyone can read the chart to discover how the process operates at each stage, which people are involved, and what kind of responsibility each has.

Figure 3.3 Deployment chart (reprinted from The Team Handbook*).*

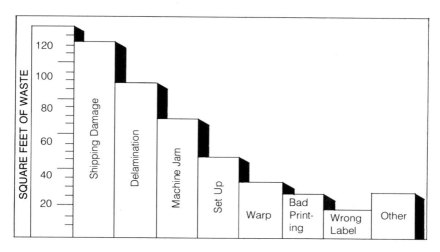

Pareto charts focus improvement efforts by ranking problems or their causes.

A Pareto chart is a series of bars whose heights reflect the frequency or impact of problems. The bars are arranged in descending order of height from left to right. This means the categories represented by the tall bars on the left are relatively more important than those on the right. The name of the chart derives from the Pareto Principle, "80% of the trouble comes from 20% of the problems." Though the percentages will never be that exact, teams usually find that most trouble comes from only a few problems.

Pareto charts are useful throughout a project: early on to identify which problem should be studied, later to narrow down which causes of the problem to address first. Since they draw everyone's attention to the "vital few" important factors where the payback is likely to be greatest, Pareto charts can be used to build consensus in a group. In general, teams should focus their attention first on the biggest problems—those with the highest bars.

***Figure 3.4** Pareto chart of materials waste (reprinted from* The Team Handbook*).*

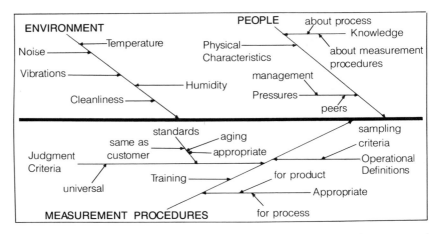

Cause-and-effect [*sic*] diagrams identify and organize possible causes of problems, or factors needed to insure success of some effort. The problem, situation, or event is listed on the right. Branches off the central arrow indicate main categories of items. Use of this format allows people to easily see the relationship between factors.

The cause-and-effect diagram, also called a "fishbone diagram" because of its appearance, allows you to map out a list of factors thought to affect a problem or desired outcome. This type of diagram was invented by Kaoru Ishikawa, and hence is also called an "Ishikawa diagram." It is an effective tool for studying processes and situations, and for planning.

A cause-and-effect diagram is essentially a pictorial display of a list. Each diagram has a large arrow pointing to the name of a problem. The branches off the large arrow represent main categories of potential causes (or solutions). Typical categories are equipment, personnel, method, materials, and environment. Teams can customize these categories to fit their processes. Smaller arrows, representing subcategories (list items), are drawn off each main branch.

Arranging lists in this way often leads to greater understanding of a problem and possible contributing factors. For example, if one category was "equipment," you could generate a list of subcategories by asking questions such as: What main equipment could be the source of the problems? What problems does this equipment have that could cause the problem we see? Similar questions can be asked for the other categories.

Since these questions lead to detailed discussions of how a process works, cause-and-effect diagrams are most effective after the process has been described and the problem well-defined. By then, team members will have a good idea of which factors to include on the diagram. When creating a cause-and-effect diagram, consult with coworkers not on the team who are familiar with various aspects of the process. This way your team will be less likely to miss important factors.

Figure 3.5 Cause and effect diagram (reprinted from The Team Handbook*).*

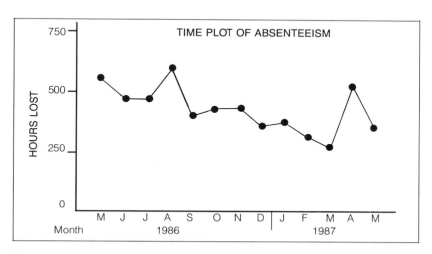

Time plots are used to examine data for trends or other patterns that occur over time. A time plot is just the data points plotted in time order.

Many factors that affect a process change over time: ingredients decay, new employees are hired, tools and equipment wear down, suppliers make changes from time to time. Any of these changes can affect data you collect from a process over time. Detecting these time-related shifts, trends, or patterns is an essential step in making long-lasting improvements. And the best way to detect the effect of these types of changes is to plot relevant measurements in time order.

When you collect data over time, the first step is to make a time plot because the presence of a time-related trend can invalidate other forms of data analysis (such as the dot plot, described on p. 2-34).

Figure 3.6 *Time plot (reprinted from* The Team Handbook*).*

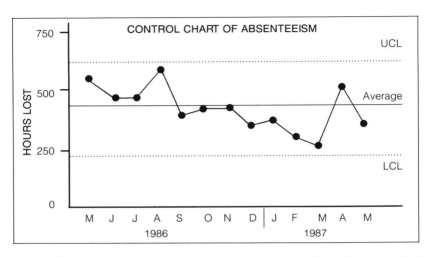

Control charts are used to monitor a process to see whether it is in statistical control. The UCL and LCL—or upper and lower control limits, respectively—indicate how much variation is typical for the process. Points that fall outside the limits or into particular patterns indicate the presence of a special cause of variation, a cause that deserves investigation.

A control chart is a time plot with one extra feature: it also indicates the range of variation built into the system. The boundaries of this range are marked by upper and lower statistical control limits, which are calculated according to statistical formulas from data collected on the process.

Control charts help you distinguish between variation inherent in a process (variation from a "common cause") and variation arising from sources that come and go unpredictably ("special causes"). Points that occur outside the control limits are signals of special causes of variation, meaning it should be relatively easy to track down that source and prevent its recurrence. Data points that stay within the control limits indicate that most variation is coming from common causes. If all points stay within the control limits, the only way to make improvements is to fundamentally change some aspect of the process (materials, procedures, equipment, training, etc.).

Figure 3.7 Control chart (reprinted from The Team Handbook).

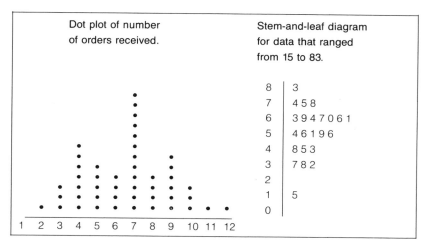

Dot plots and stem-and-leaf displays show which values occur and how often and can be used to quickly check the distribution, or spread, of the data.

A dot plot starts as a line marked off in units corresponding to data measurement. A dot is then placed above a value for each time that value appeared in the data. Dot plots are easily constructed, display all the data points, and readily convey information. A quick look at one tells you right away the range of measurements you found, what the central value or average is, and how data points are distributed around the average (whether they are symmetric or not). Sometimes they are used to get a quick look at data before further analysis. Any data plotted on a time plot is usually converted to a dot plot to watch the distribution (spread of points) as well as the pattern over time. Note: do not make a dot plot of data that shows time-related patterns. In many cases, the plotted points will fall into the outline of a bell, a shape familiar to statisticians. The bell is formed by a natural tendency in data points to cluster about a central value (called the ''average'' or ''mean'') and taper off symmetrically on both sides. Other times they may show abnormal data patterns such as those caused by error or inspector bias.

A stem-and-leaf diagram is a minor variation on the dot plot. Here, a line (or ''stem'') is drawn vertically, and the units that would be marked below the line on a dot plot are put on the left of this line. The rest of the digits from the actual measurements are entered on the corresponding rows. For example, in the diagram shown above, the units of ten are shown on the left side of the stem, and the units of one are on the right.

The advantage of stem-and-leaf diagrams over the dot plot is that you can easily reproduce the actual measurements; in a dot plot you may have trouble deciding at a later time exactly where the measurement fell. However, as shown in the examples above, dot plots work well where there are many repeated values.

Figure 3.8 *Dot plots and stem-and-leaf displays (reprinted from* The Team Handbook*)*.

A simple checksheet for monitoring damage to shipping cartons.

Place a check where you observe carton damage.

Date _____

Shift _____

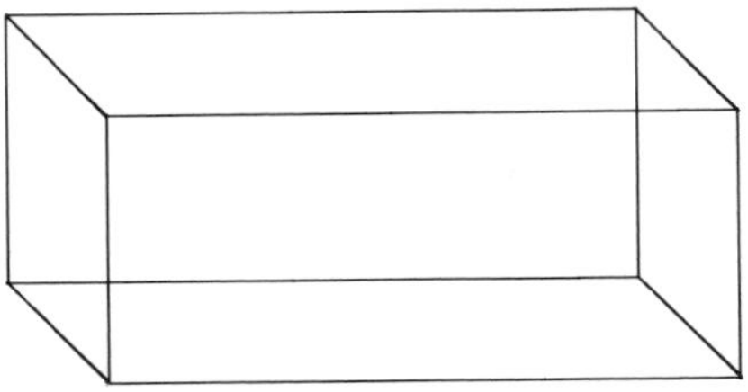

Process Step
(check one)
___ warehouse
___ mfg/assembly
___ packaging
___ storage
___ shipping

Checksheets are structured forms that make it easy to record and analyze data. They are therefore used in every project stage that includes data collection—so we could have put them anywhere in our sequence and been correct. The best checksheets are simple to use, make use of your operational definitions, and visually display the data in a format that can reveal underlying patterns.

Here are some hints that will make your checksheets more effective:

- Incorporating a visual element is an extremely useful trick because it lets you get information from the data without having to do any calculations. For instance, if you are collecting information on the number of errors made on a form, consider making check marks right on copies of the form. That way you can instantly know both how many times an error occurred and whether its position on the form affects how easy it is to pick out. Sketches of a product being checked can also simplify data collection.
- Make sure data collectors will interpret the check-off categories in the same way, using agreed-upon operational definitions—if they don't, the data will probably be useless.
- Keep sheets separately for different days, different operators, and so on. That way you will be able to look for patterns related to time or sequence as well as patterns related to differences in operators and other factors.
- Test the checksheets before a project begins, and make improvements as you see necessary.

Figure 3.9 Checksheet (reprinted from The Team Handbook*).*

44

perform their own tasks in such a way that it will make it easier for co-workers to do their jobs in a quality fashion.

Quality Characteristic 7—The Use of Human Sensors

Gauges are more accurate than humans. As a General Electric quality officer said to me, "you can't give people 20/20 vision." Gauges don't have bad emotional times, or hangovers, or all the other emotions that affect the performance of human beings. Therefore, quality is less predictable if human sensing is required.

However, when the quality movement entered into the service industries and into other types of production that could not be measured by a gauge or other artificial means, human sensing became a common means of measuring quality. Under the old system of quality control, which was based totally on specifications, units of measure, strict tolerances, and sensing devices, the use of human sensors was avoided if at all possible. But under the current management philosophy, which has replaced strict tolerances with the concept of continuous improvement, the use of human sensors has increased.

Today industry relies on human sensing for the continuous improvement of quality. Industries spend enormous time, energy, and resources to improve the human sensing. Their efforts center more on the affective domain, i.e., attitude, ownership, caring, pride, etc., than on the cognitive knowledge needed to perform the sensor operation. The operation can be learned quickly. The desire to do the job right seems more important to industry in their staff development process.

Quality Characteristic 8—Quality Teams

In industry today, there is widespread use of teams to address quality issues and solve quality problems. These teams are made up of representatives from all levels of the organization—that is, line management, staff support people, and the workforce, or the people doing the actual operations.

This teaming concept centers around a new style of management called total quality management or quality leadership. It is a view that shifts the emphasis from profits to quality. It is not based on the elimination of profits, which is a primary reason why private industry exists.

It is based on the belief that emphasizing quality will, in the long run, provide more and more lasting profits.

The concept has another significant shift in industrial thinking—that is, the shift from product to process emphasis. The new focus is on improving how work gets done (the methods), instead of what is done (the results).

The dominant purpose of the teamwork is an attempt to break down the barriers, rivalries, and distrust that currently exists between and among management, workers, and their representatives. The goal is to create partnerships among all the levels of the organization. This partnership will then pursue the common struggle for customers, and discontinue the common struggle for power. This notion of the common struggle for customers applies to relationships with suppliers, regulating agencies, and local communities.

This team approach to quality puts all members of the organization, not just management, into the identification, diagnosis, and solving of quality issues and problems. Therefore, the lines of communication change dramatically. Communication is no longer dominated by downward communication based on hierarchical positions, but is characterized also by upward communication from workers to management, and cross communication among all groups in multiple directions.

My interviews and observations of the use of quality teams, as defined in this work, compel me to conclude that, at the present time, the use of this concept is more prevalent in management than in the workforce. So far, the unions have not entirely bought into the concept. It is easy to conjecture why this could be the case. For instance there may have been a long history of management/union unrest or conflict. Or perhaps the union sees its traditional role being undermined by the new management philosophy. Perhaps the union even views the quality team as a threat to its continued existence. The point is, my research indicated that the implementation of this concept is as much a goal as it is a reality. In all cases, however, there is a discernible movement toward the total implementation.

The management strategy that seemed to be the most prevalent in attempting to totally employ the team approach to quality was the use of role modeling. Universally, the management personnel that I interviewed stated that if management continues to role model the team approach, the workers and the workers' unions will eventually buy into the concept.

Quality Characteristic 9—Flattening the Hierarchy

The movement in industry to flatten out the hierarchy to improve quality has had multiple results. They are:

- The elimination of outside inspection functions has reduced the number of middle management positions.
- The inclusion of workers in the quality process has reduced the number of middle management positions.
- The desire to ease and improve communications has led companies to reduce the levels of the hierarchy.

All of these results are based on the company's desire to improve quality. They are all part of the new management philosophy that emphasizes self inspection and total quality management. However, my research leads me to believe that there are also economic motives involved in flattening the hierarchy. High salaries, fringe benefits, and insurance costs are being cut by private enterprise. Industries are now attempting to divert more resources to the actual productivity operation. Their examination of foreign competition, especially Japan, revealed that American industry was employing far more middle management than their more successful foreign competition.

Quality Characteristic 10—Natural Work Groups

In the "old days" of quality control and quality assurance, the following dialogue was common. You could even say it was the state of affairs in private industry. Worker to production foreman or supervisor: "I've got a quality problem." Supervisor's response: "You got a quality problem. Call quality control."

Production and quality were separate functions, organized separately and administered separately. The production department had one goal: production quotas. The quality control department had another goal: maintaining quality standards. One goal involved quantity; the other quality. Oftentimes, the goals conflicted. Always, eventually, both production and quality people had to become involved in the solving of quality problems and the maintenance of quality standards.

Under this organizational structure, the natural work for production personnel was to meet production quotas. The natural work for quality personnel was to inspect the work of the production people to insure that quality standards were being maintained. For production people to have to become involved in quality problems or processes was not part of their work function. It was beyond the call of duty, so to speak. It interfered with their goal, which was the production quota. Quality people set and maintained the standards, from an exterior perspective. The enhancement or interference with production quotas was not their function. Only quality concerned them.

This approach is perceived today by industry as passé thinking. It led to competitiveness, jealousy, noncooperation, and poor quality. It is being rapidly replaced by natural work groups. Natural work groups are based on the premise that quality is everyone's job. Natural work groups are a cross section of the company, including management, production, quality, and other departments. They are created to work on a problem or an improvement effort. The cross section must include people at the operations level, as well as engineers, managers, or other personnel who could contribute to the decision-making process.

Work on quality pursuits or topics is part of the natural job of the people involved, regardless of their operational function. In other words, it is not extracurricular. If a production worker is asked to work on a quality problem, two things will occur. One, someone else will do the production work he/she normally performs. Two, the quality problem will be worked on during regular hours. In other words, the production worker does not take on additional duties or work to perform the quality function.

Another significant part of natural work groups is that training for all the participants is provided. Industry realizes that group problem solving has some prerequisites. Therefore, the training of personnel is part of the natural work process also. This staff or professional development involves whatever skills are needed. The most common center around communication, interpersonal relationships, teaming strategies, problem solving, critical thinking, and information on the process or product being studied.

Quality Characteristic 11—Empowerment

This is being accomplished through the concept of building quality into the work process, and relying less and less on outside inspection. If you are going to make people responsible for their own quality, you are going to be empowering them. This empowerment will automatically mean a reduction in top down management.

Private enterprise is empowering the workers by first making them responsible for the quality of their work. This is positional or job empowerment. The intent is to make workers into quality inspectors of their own work, and thus reduce the need for external inspection. This automatically moves quality toward process emphasis and away from product emphasis.

Personal job empowerment is also occurring. Personal empowerment means that, as a person, the worker is (1) free to take more responsibility, and (2) valued for his/her opinion on all matters relative to the company's operation. Also, a worker's opinion will receive equal consideration with those of all levels of management.

Two examples of empowerment are (1) that any assembly line worker may stop the production line operation if he/she sees a breach of quality, and (2) employee suggestion programs solicit and utilize employee suggestions regardless of the level or position of the person making the suggestion.

Quality Characteristic 12—Abandonment

As competition has become keener, companies have begun to break down their operations to see where losses are occurring. Then they are abandoning those operations for the sake of financial survival.

However, abandonment in industry is also occurring as an attempt to maintain organizational clarity, focus, and constancy of purpose. Recent decades have seen numerous mergers and takeovers in large industries. These consolidations have produced some interesting results that demonstrate the need for abandonment systems.

Many of the mergers have been between two successful companies who decided that they could be even more successful if they merged. Both companies were profitable, and a merger would theoretically double their profits. An interesting thing happened on their way to the bank—two separate successful companies became one unsuccessful company. The new, bigger company, began to lose profits, even to the point of losing money. It was discovered that the two separate companies, who had each possessed focus and constancy of purpose as individual enterprises, lost that focus as a result of the merger. Although each was successful, they were successful in different ways, with different management philosophies. The new company had too many goals, products, missions, and focus.

In today's highly competitive quality market, companies are finding that the abandonment of unsuccessful aspects of the company is a road to quality and thus profits. Growth is no longer the only way to improvement. Abandonment has become another avenue, an avenue that works toward focus and constancy of purpose—a prerequisite to quality.

A second type of abandonment that is occurring in the private sector is in management philosophy, specifically in the level and use of middle management. Basically, there has been a change in the functions of middle management and a reduction in its workforce. These changes reflect the decreasing dependence on outside inspection in the pursuit of quality. The specific personnel changes that are occurring are (1) a reduction in line management, (2) a transfer of line management personnel to productivity positions (both 1 and 2 are described by industry as the elimination of excess middle management, and are perceived as part of their drive to become "leaner and meaner"), and (3) the merging of productivity and quality functions has led to the abandonment of quality control departments.

The "rule of thumb" that the companies are following with regard to the abandonment of middle management is that middle management personnel must be involved in the productivity process, must perform a resource service that is necessary for increased productivity/quality, or be in a line management position that makes meaningful/necessary decisions.

There is no question that the abandonment of middle management positions in industry has also been pursued to cut costs on salaries and to cut excessive medical costs, both of which were driving companies out of business. So the abandonment process has been both the result of management philosophy and a cost-cutting measure made necessary by the tough international competition that currently exists in most industries.

The "frontier philosophy" of American industry, built on the concept of perpetual growth as the means to prosperity and excellence, has been joined by abandonment of unprofitable operations and personnel as a means of pursuing improvement. Companies have begun abandoning those operations and processes that are not profitable, and therefore have eliminated people not contributing to productivity/quality. Peter Drucker once said, "American organizations have no systematic way of abandoning anything." American companies have realized this and are working toward abandonment as a means of improvement. No longer is abandonment seen as an indication of an unhealthy or unprofitable company on its way to bankruptcy.

Quality Characteristic 13—Reduction in Inspection

Industry is moving away from management inspection and monitoring of workers and toward self responsibility for the quality of work. This is a movement away from the pipeline model of Shewhart (see Figure 2.1). The pipeline notion held that there were three steps in the quality control process: the specification of what is wanted, the production of things to satisfy the specification, and the inspection of the things produced to see if they satisfy the specification. In educational terms, the specification could be thought of as the curriculum, the production as the instruction, and inspection as testing or assessment. Under the old notion of production, these three steps were thought of as independent. One could specify what was wanted, someone else could take this specification as a guide and make the product, and an inspector could measure the product to see if it met specifications. This worldview grew out of the manufacturing experiences of the 1800s, and is still seen in various roles today, including that of education. The lack of feedback from steps two and three to step one results in a specification-driven approach to productivity.

The purpose of inspection was to separate the "good stuff" from the bad, and efforts were focused on improving the sorting process. Too little thought was focused on the improvement of the process, because of the amount of time and energy required for the inspection operation.

What industry has found is that inspection is too late, too expensive, and though it catches scrap, it does not prevent it. The pipeline model also takes away quality responsibility from the person doing the operation. This state of affairs is characterized by the following phrase: "You got a quality problem, let quality control fix it; your job is production."

Quality systems in industry have moved away from the pipeline model to cyclic models (see Figure 2.2). The new model interlinks the steps of specification, production, and inspection. It places the responsibility for all three steps on the operator and thus reduces the need for outside inspection and monitoring. These systems are referred to today in many industries as the total quality approach or system. The byword is, do it right the first time, or, do it till you get it right. And, of course, the most significant aspect of the new approach is the trust in and reliance upon the person doing the work, not an outside inspector.

Quality Characteristic 14—Change in Management Philosophy

When I began this research into the quality efforts of private industry I expected to find heavy emphasis on statistical standards, specifications, units of measure, and sensors: in other words, the statistical tools for accountability. Although I have found that these tools are being used, I did not find them to be at the heart of industry's efforts to improve quality, either in the product or service sphere. Instead, I found that private industry is attempting to improve quality through new management philosophies. The attitude I found among the leadership of the companies I researched was that the "old way" of approaching quality by using command and control through statistics and inspection was not working in the new international market. I found that they were attempting to improve quality by applying new management philosophies and theories.

If forced to sum up these management changes in one word, I would say "Deming." Amazingly, although agreement with the total Deming philosophy was not present, all the company executives that I researched and interviewed mentioned the Deming principles as integral to their current quality efforts. They do adapt the Deming points to their different industries, but they all supported the "Deming way" as a part of their company's management efforts.

The Deming management method is summarized in his famous "fourteen points" listed below.[14]

(1) Constancy of purpose

(2) Adopt a new philosophy

(3) Cease mass inspection

(4) End price tag business

(5) Improve constantly (production and service)

[14]Deming, W. E. 1991. *Out of the Crisis*. Cambridge, MA: Massachusetts Institute of Technology, Center for Advanced Engineering Study, p. 24.

(6) Institute training/retraining

(7) Institute leadership

(8) Drive out fear

(9) Break down departmental barriers

(10) Eliminate slogans, targets

(11) Eliminate numerical quotas

(12) Remove barriers to worker pride

(13) Institute education/self-improvement

(14) Transformation

Let's examine each of these points individually.

Deming Point 1—Constancy of Purpose

Management has two sets of problems—today's and tomorrow's. The problems of today concern the immediate needs of the company—how to maintain quality, budgets, employment, and public relations. Most American companies dwell on these types of problems, without adequate attention to the future. Because corporate managers change jobs every two or three years, their interests are short term. They live for the next quarter dividend. This short-term view is not conducive to constancy of purpose.

Establishing constancy of purpose means (1) innovation; (2) research and education; (3) maintenance of equipment, furniture and fixtures, and new aids to production in the office and the plant.

Innovation does not consist of the introduction of some flashy new product or process for the mere sake of having something new to sell. The product or service must have a market and be able to help people in some way.

Before a company proceeds with any innovation, it should address the following questions and have a plan for each:

- What materials will be required and at what cost?
- What will be the method of production?
- What new people will have to be hired?
- What changes in equipment will be required?
- What new skills will be required, and for how many people?
- How will current employees be trained in these new skills?
- How will supervisors be trained?

- What will be the cost of production?
- What will be the cost of marketing?
- What will be the cost and method of service?
- How will the product or service be used by the client?
- How will the company know if the customer (client) is satisfied?

To prepare for the future, companies must invest today. There can be no innovation without research, and no research without properly educated employees. Companies must put significant resources into research efforts.

Continuous improvement of product and service is a significant aspect of constancy of purpose. Companies can go "down the tube," making the wrong product or providing the wrong service, even though everyone in the organization performs with devotion, employing statistical methods and every other aid that can boost efficiency.

Last of all, a company must invest in the maintenance of equipment, and introduce new equipment to replace outdated machinery. Otherwise, the future is not possible, and thus, staying in business is not possible.

Deming Point 2—Adopt a New Philosophy

Quality has become the new religion. We are in a new economic age based on international competition. Western management must awaken to this challenge. Japan has introduced a new economic age of reliability and smooth operation. Deming says that where America has been beaten is in management. So the term "new philosophy," as used in current industrial literature, refers to a new philosophy of management.

In the post World War Two era, the United States dominated the markets of the world. We felt that our dominance was due to our competence when in reality our dominance was due to the lack of competition. World War Two had devastated both Europe and Japan. This fact became all too clear when Japan began invading our markets successfully with top-quality products.

Faced with this new and stiff competition, American industry has begun to utilize a new philosophy of management that is quality-based and derived from customer or client satisfaction.

Deming Point 3—Cease Mass Inspection

The "old way" was to inspect bad quality out. The "new way" is to build good quality in. Said another way, the current quality methods of industry are to make every attempt to eliminate the need for inspection by building quality into the product or process. Inspection that has the aim of trying to find the bad ones is too late, ineffective, and costly.

When inspection is necessary, it is considered a way to find out what the company is doing right. Also, there is tremendous effort to see that the inspection is carried out in a professional manner, and not by "lick and spit" methods.

It seems to be the goal of industry to totally eliminate the need for inspection. The entire emphasis has switched to more training and responsibility for self inspection and correction by the operator or worker.

Central to this Deming point is what he calls the absurdity of meeting specifications as a means of achieving quality. Within the concept of specifications is the term "tolerances." If a product is within tolerances, which is the amount of error a product may have and still pass inspection, it is considered to be of sufficient quality to be sold. The Japanese exploited this American quality method by continually reducing the tolerance and emphasizing continual improvement.

Inspection was traditionally used to check parts or products to see that they were within specifications. Unfortunately, in today's international market, just being within specifications does not ensure sufficient quality to meet customer satisfaction. Why buy less than perfect products if perfect ones are on the market? Perfect products, those with zero tolerance, can only be achieved at the operator level, not by means of a random or total inspection that occurs after the fact.

Deming Point 4—End Price Tag Business

This Deming point mainly refers to the relationship between companies and their suppliers or vendors. Deming claims that using low bidding as a basis for business creates a situation of jumping from vendor to vendor which, in turn, creates increased reliance on the use of specifications to produce quality products.

Deming claims that this reliance on specifications, manuals full of standards, and the inspection of incoming parts or products is not conducive to quality. He feels that by developing a long-term relationship with fewer vendors, quality would be better served. This relationship would be built on loyalty and trust. It would involve the suppliers spending time on the floor of the manufacturing plant of the company to see how their products fit into the overall process of their customer. The company would spend time in the plants of the suppliers in order to train their workers in their expectations, and assist in solving problems that arise.

Even though this long-term partnership will require talent and manpower, in the long run, it will save money and improve quality by eliminating the need for mass inspection of incoming parts and products.

Deming Point 5—Improve Constantly (Production and Service)

This point emphasizes that improvement is not a one-time effort. It emphasizes that constant improvement is not like fire fighting, but is based on quality and productivity. Deming puts the onus on management to achieve this point. Management is obligated to improve continually, because only management can initiate improvement in quality.

Statistical thinking is important to this quality point. Only by the use of properly interpreted data can intelligent decisions be made. But to depend only on the use of statistics is a sure way to go out of business. Also, remember that meeting specifications only insures the status quo.

Supplement statistical data with the following questions:

(1) Are you doing better than a year ago?
(2) Are you doing better than five years ago?
(3) Is your marketing more effective?
(4) Has client satisfaction increased?
(5) Has pride and performance of employees improved?

Deming Point 6—Institute Training/Retraining

This point centers on the training of workers and is based on the premise that training should occur only until statistical control is achieved. The training would consist of knowledge of the significance of variation and a rudimentary knowledge of control charts. Deming also points out that the weakness of most training programs in industry is that workers are teaching workers and that such training is limited to a knowledge of what they are doing, without regard to whether it is right or wrong. As time goes on, the training gets worse and worse. He equates it to whispering a fact around the room from one person to another. By the time it reaches the end it is much less accurate than when it started.

Deming Point 7—Institute Leadership

Leadership should be the job of management. Its aim should be to help people do a good job. The point centers around the concept of supervision. Deming says that supervisors today never did the work they supervise, therefore they know less than the workers and cannot help them with problems. So no leadership is happening. He goes so far as to say that if supervisors can't help, they shouldn't exist.

Deming Point 8—Drive Out Fear

Management is afraid to ask questions, or take positions, or point out problems for fear of being blamed. No incentives exist to expose problems. New ideas are risky because they could cause the loss of raises, promotions, jobs, punitive assignments. These are the elements of fear that Deming says companies must eliminate.

Fear robs people of their chance to contribute to the company. It is necessary for people to feel secure if they are expected to contribute to quality efforts. According to Deming, fear will disappear as people develop confidence in management.

Deming Point 9—Break Down Departmental Barriers

When departments don't work together, even superb departmental efforts may not guarantee success. People in research, design, sales, and production must work as a team, to foresee problems in both production and customer use. Goals must not conflict, or they can ruin the company.

It is the job of management to help departments work together and to promote teamwork. Deming says that companies must change their system before this can be done. He points out that when the showdown comes under the present system and someone has to decide between his own rating or the company's, he will decide for himself. He also asks, "Can you blame him?"

Deming Point 10—Eliminate Slogans, Targets, and Exhortations

Such exhortations as these only create adversarial relationships, as the bulk of the causes of low quality and low productivity belong to the system and thus lie beyond the power of the workforce.

Slogans are based on the belief that people could, if they tried, do better. People are offended, not inspired by them. Deming makes the point that all of these ideas are based on a goal without regard to the means that will result in its accomplishment. Deming states that the way to improvement is through management's efforts to change the system so that workers can do quality work.

Deming Point 11—Eliminate Numerical Quotas

This point urges the elimination of management by numbers, numerical goals, and objectives. It recommends that they be replaced with what Deming calls leadership. He claims that quotas impede quality by setting productivity levels. Everybody meets these levels or quotas and then quits, succumbing to either peer pressure or competency level. Everyone regresses toward the quota.

Quotas should be replaced by a system that fosters an atmosphere of receptivity and recognition, which enhances the feeling of loyalty and pride at having ideas accepted. This type of system is preferable to one that measures people by the numbers that they turn out.

Deming Point 12—Remove Barriers to Worker Pride

Deming exhorts us to quit treating people as commodities, to be used as needed and then discarded. Instead, invest them with more authority and trust and act more on their decisions and recommendations. He claims that people are basically motivated, but the system does not allow them the freedom to act on their motivation. Therefore, many have lost, at least temporarily, interest in their job. Key to achieving this point is that yearly merit rating schemes and management by objectives must be eliminated.

Deming Point 13—Institute Education/Self-Improvement

It is not enough to have good people in your organization. They must be continually acquiring new knowledge and skills in methods.

Education and training must fit people into new jobs and responsibilities.

Deming Point 14—Putting Everyone to Work, to Realize the Transformation

This point means that management will have to organize teams to accomplish the transformation. The transformation is everybody's job, and involves four steps (see Figure 2.3).

In addition to the Shewhart cycle, everyone needs to begin to think of his/her work from the perspective of customer satisfaction, both internal and external. Ask yourself, who is the person who receives your work?

A critical mass is necessary for this point. Everyone in the organization must understand the fourteen points and how they work. Management must see that this is accomplished.

Education is at least as well equipped as business and industry to get everyone involved in a transformation to a quality approach involving Deming's fourteen points. In view of the large percentage of professionally trained personnel available to schools, only a change in management philosophy is needed.

Dr. Deming also notes *diseases* and *obstacles* that stand in the way of the quality transformation.[15] Diseases are serious and obstacles are not quite as serious.

The Seven Deadly Diseases

(1) Lack of constancy of purpose

(2) Emphasis on short-term profits

(3) Evaluation of performance, merit rating, or annual review

(4) Mobility of top management

(5) Running the company on visible figures alone

(6) Excessive medical costs

(7) Excessive costs of warranty, fueled by lawyers who work on contingency fees

[15]Ibid., p. 97.

Obstacles

- neglect of long-range planning and transformation
- the supposition that solving problems, automation, gadgets, and new machinery will transform industry
- search for examples
- the sense that "our problems are different"
- obsolescence in schools
- reliance on quality control departments
- blaming the workforce for problems
- quality by inspection
- false starts
- the unmanned computer
- meeting specifications
- inadequate testing of prototypes
- an attitude of "anyone who comes to help us must understand everything about our business"

Quality Characteristic 15—The 85/15 Rule

Current quality leadership thinking recognizes, as Dr. Joseph M. Juran and Dr. W. Edwards Deming have maintained since the early 1950s, that at least 85 percent of an organization's failures are the fault of management-controlled systems.[16] Workers can control no more than 15 percent of the problems. In quality leadership as practiced by industry, the focus is on constant and rigorous improvement of every system, not on blaming individuals for problems.

This current approach to problem solving refutes the widely held belief that an organization would have few, if any, problems if only workers would do their jobs correctly. As Juran pointed out many years ago, this belief is incorrect.

In fact, the potential to eliminate mistakes and errors lies mostly in improving the systems through which work is done, not in changing the workers.

Even in cases where it does appear that an individual is doing something wrong, often the trouble lies in how that worker was trained, which is a system problem.

---

[16]Juran, J. M. and F. M. Gryna, Jr. 1980. *Quality Planning & Analysis*. New York, NY: McGraw-Hill, p. 139.

Once people recognize that systems create the majority of problems, they will stop blaming individual workers. They will instead ask which system needs improving, and will be more likely to seek out and find the true source of the problem.

Quality Characteristic 16—Quality as a People Issue

One of the initial stages of this research was to interview people in industry who were responsible for the quality efforts in their company of employment. In my first interview, at a major machine tool and plastics machine manufacturer, I asked a question that contained the term *quality control*. He informed me that if I came to talk about quality control, he could be of little help. He had not heard the term used for at least ten years in industrial circles among informed people. He explained to me that the term *quality control* had been replaced by the term *quality assurance*. However, both are now obsolete. The new terms are *quality systems* or *corporate quality* or *total quality* or other terms that indicate that quality is not something you control, but something that is inherent in the work itself.[17]

What I consistently found in my research of the quality efforts of eight major companies is that industry has found that quality, on a work-competitiveness basis, cannot be achieved through the traditional quality control approach. That approach involves setting artificial standards, specifications, units of measure, tolerances, and inspections. Instead, the approach is universally one of total quality involving all levels of the company from the president to the operators. The standard is continuous improvement, to achieve quality based on the definition of meeting and exceeding clients' needs and expectations.

To accomplish this, the companies are working toward changing people's behavior. This effort centers around personal improvement through individual growth plans and team efforts like project teams, guidance teams, and natural work groups.

This personal improvement is pursued as part of the natural work process. Therefore, it is done during the regular workday, and the normal work duties are assigned to someone else. Other characteristics of the training are: (1) interpersonal communications skills and techniques, (2) defining specific skills needed for each job and providing the training based on those needs, (3) using real work situations in

[17]Saylor, M. Corporate Director, Quality Standards and Certification, Cincinnati Milicron, Cincinnati, Ohio. Interview, 14 Dec., 1990.

training, (4) reinforcing training at work immediately, and (5) all training is predicated on the need to educate people for a changing workplace and new roles.

Quality Characteristic 17—Employee Suggestion Program

Companies have begun formal programs designed to solicit and process employees' ideas and put the good ones to work. It is a type of collegial support system.

At this point in time, the programs have not reached the level of participation that the companies had hoped. For example, in Japan, companies receive an average of twenty-two suggestions per year from each employee. In the United States, the average is only .02 suggestions per employee per year.[18]

It seems that this discrepancy in participation between Japan and the United States is cultural in nature. Employee participation doesn't have the history of use in the United States as it does in Japan, and it is not a part of the natural work process in America, either. Americans believe that some people are paid to work, others are paid to think. That mindset must be eliminated before employee suggestion programs become a major component of the quality movement.

SUMMARY

All of the quality characteristics discussed in this chapter, including W. Edwards Deming's fourteen points, are derived from the most up-to-date quality practices currently at work in industry. Together they make up the movement known as total quality management, which is geared toward bringing American industry back from its doldrums and making it competitive again in the international arena. This movement focuses less on machines than on the people who run the machines, less on numerical standards and more on the elusive though all-important notion of quality. In the next few chapters, we will examine how each of these quality characteristics applies to American education, and we will attempt to determine whether a movement that has been proved to raise the quality of American industrial products can truly be used to raise the quality of American students.

[18]Kuhr, S. Quality Assurance Advisor, AT&T, Cincinnati, Ohio. Interview, 20 Dec., 1990.

THE APPLICATION OF TOTAL QUALITY MANAGEMENT PRINCIPLES TO SCHOOL MANAGEMENT

In Part Two, the concept of total quality management is applied to the management of America's schools. The quality characteristics that were derived from industry in Part One will be examined in greater detail, in order to determine whether they can be translated to the educational sphere—and if so, how.

Chapter 4 provides a workable definition of quality, and discusses quality characteristic 1—a continuous improvement standard, in regard to education.

Chapter 5 deals with the subject of organizational focus, and discusses quality characteristics 2 through 4—the use of consumer research, the external quality concept, and quality function deployment.

Chapter 6 discusses how one can and cannot measure progress in schools, addressing quality characteristics 5 through 7—statistical process control, the internal quality concept, and the use of human sensors.

Chapter 7 examines how schools can reallocate resources to pursue a program of total quality management. To this end, it discusses quality characteristics 8 through 13—quality teams, flattening the hierarchy, natural work groups, empowerment, abandonment, and reduction in inspection.

Chapter 8 outlines the total quality management philosophy that schools will have to adopt if they seek real change, beginning with a look at quality characteristic 14—change in management philosophy, focusing particularly on Deming's fourteen points and their application to education. From there, the chapter goes on to examine quality char-

acteristics 15 through 17—the 85/15 rule, quality as a people issue, and the employee suggestion program.

Chapter 9 concludes the book with a look at putting total quality management to work in schools. The result is a system that will bring quality to the forefront of American education, just as it is now being brought to the forefront of American industry.

CHAPTER 4 ||||||||||||||||||||||||||||||||||||||||||||||||||||||||||||||||||||||||||||||||||||||||||||||||||||||||||||||||||||||||||||||||||||||||||

Client Satisfaction (The Quality Definition) and Continuous Improvement (The Quality Standard)

APPLICATION OF THE DEFINITION

It is impossible to discuss quality management without first knowing what is meant by *quality*.

The operational definition of quality being used in this book is simply this—quality is determined by the client. Quality is accomplished by continually meeting and exceeding client needs and expectations at a price they are willing to pay. Price in this educational context means the willingness of the clients to support public and private schools through self-imposed taxes, tuition, and other costs.

The usefulness of this definition depends on the proper identification of who are the clients for schools. Unlike many manufacturers and other service industries, schools have more than one client. In fact, they have two primary clients—parents/guardians, and students. They also have two secondary clients—future employers of their current students, and the higher education institutions that will receive some of their graduates.

The primary clients should be viewed from the external quality perspective, which asks the question, "Are we continually meeting and exceeding the needs and expectations of the clients at a price they are willing to pay?" The parents or guardians are defined as whoever is sending the student to school. The same perspective is applied to students. Of course, the more choices that parents and students have, the more like clients they become. With more choices available to clients, schools must make a greater attempt to meet their needs and expectations.

One of the most interesting aspects of attempting to apply the concept of quality to schools is identifying the role of students. In essence,

65

students can be viewed as performing multiple roles. They are the clients, a role which, as was previously stated, will become more acute as choices increase. Students are also the workers. Perhaps most significant of all, from the accountability viewpoint, they are the products of the school.

The fact that they are both the workers and the products of the school makes the application of industrial quality concepts difficult. This is a situation unique to education. Even if you view the school as a service industry, which I do, the situation of the school is still unique. Other service industries serve up hamburgers, or advice, or comfort, or other things. The commonality that all the other service industries have is that their product, their service, is not the worker. But in education, students are the only product. This dual role does not make the application of quality impossible, it simply requires the acceptance that the dual role of students as workers and products does not prohibit the concept's application.

The secondary clients, future employers and higher education institutions, are viewed from the perspective of the internal quality principle. The key question in the application of internal quality is, "What can I do that will make your job easier and thus, more effective?" To do this, according to total quality principles and experience, schools, universities, and employers need to walk a mile in each other's shoes. That means that they should do actual work in each other's workplace so that an intelligent and informed response can be applied to the question, "What can I do to make your job more effective?"

Needless to say, the whole purpose of pursuing internal quality with universities is to increase the chances of your graduates being accepted into the universities and doing well once they get there. With employers, you want to increase the possibility that they will employ your graduates, and that your graduates will have success once they are on the job.

Just the fact that schools have identified their clients does not suffice for total quality management. Schools already have clients. Somehow, schools must identify and pursue client satisfaction. The term *satisfaction* indicates that the client has some kind of choice. The term *choice* indicates that the client is involved with decision making. This decision making must be focused on some aspect of the educational program. What is being pursued here is educational quality, not efficiency in transportation, food, or sports.

The simplest, cleanest application of total quality management to education would be unrestricted parental choice. However, that extreme is not necessary for schools to initiate total quality management. The constant for total quality management is that some choice or decision is available for the external clients. It will not suffice for a school to say to its clients that there are no choices or decisions for them to make. By the very definition of quality, clients must be able to register their satisfaction through choice and decision making. Anything less will not satisfy the operational definition of total quality.

Other client options that would satisfy the definition of total quality short of an absolute voucher system would be a choice of schools within a district, a choice of programs within a district, a choice of programs within a building, a choice of teachers within a program, magnet or alternative schools, or programs within one district or through a consortium of districts.

One of the interesting questions about the application of total quality to schools is this: must schools provide a choice that involves two identical programs? Some would argue yes. They would say that otherwise, choice is not involved. I disagree. Providing alternative programs, each designed to meet the needs and expectations of particular types of students, does provide the choice necessary for client satisfaction.

After all, car companies produce many models, each designed to meet the economic and traveling needs of different clients. Restaurants offer menus that vary in price and content. The key consideration is that a school offer enough options or alternatives that it can reasonably expect to fulfill the operational definition of meeting and exceeding clients' expectations.

The nature of schooling, and the restrictions that this nature imposes, creates certain constraints with regard to the pursuit of client satisfaction. Remember, children are involved. This fact limits the amount of transportation and distance that is tolerable to the family unit. A person could buy a car from anywhere. Once the car reaches its destination, the place of its manufacture is a moot point. But choosing a school for a youngster involves certain obstacles and constraints. These human considerations will enter into the decision on the options available. But they will not prevent the parent/guardian from exercising judgments. This model, which is based on total quality thinking, changes the role of the client from input and throughput to judgment. The professionals plan and implement programs. The clients pass judgment and act accordingly. Acting accordingly means assessing their level of satisfaction with the quality of their chosen program and making decisions about their continued involvement and support.

QUALITY CHARACTERISTIC 1—A CONTINUOUS IMPROVEMENT STANDARD

Historically, a quality control program was based on standards that were quantifiable. These standards were fixed. If the process or product stayed within the standard's allowable tolerance, then the expected level of quality was considered adequate. Such thinking is obsolete. Total quality management is based on *the standard of continuous improvement*. As we now proceed through the remaining chapters, quality characteristics, which represent the total quality process, will be applied to education. Keep in mind that the standard for each of these quality characteristics is *continuous improvement*. Therefore, the standards are not fixed, and neither are the tolerances. The aim is continuous improvement.

The use of continuous improvement as the standard for total quality management for schools makes the idea of "quality schools" feasible and viable. The school's products are people. The variance in people's intellectual, physical, emotional, and environmental makeup is significant, so that fixed standards and tolerances simply are not feasible. But continuous improvement is not only feasible, it is also measurable and quantifiable. Instead of establishing arbitrary standards and measuring against these standards year after year, total quality management will establish a baseline of data and information and begin attempting to improve upon it continuously.

Schools using the principle of continuous improvement as their quality index would begin by establishing baseline data from which to measure their yearly improvement. This baseline data should be established for all indicators of quality that the school is going to use to evaluate its continuous improvement. Areas that are certain to be included are:

(1) Student norm-referenced test scores
(2) Student criterion-referenced test scores
(3) Student attendance figures

(4) Staff attendance figures

(5) Parental involvement

(6) Follow-up information on students, such as success rate in college or employment

(7) Rate of staff turnover

The primary and secondary clients of the school should have substantial input into what the continuous improvement indicators are going to be. Therefore, students and parents, the primary clients, and colleges and employers, the secondary clients, should be involved in this process.

Schools using continuous improvement would not set new product goals every year. The goal would be continuous improvement in all the areas decided on as quality indicators. There would be process goals that could be used to assist in the process of continuous improvement.

The use of the industrial model of continuous improvement has some obvious benefits to education. It would get schools out of the inevitable comparisons with other schools based on test results, which tend to reflect the socioeconomic status of the communities instead of performance measurement based on student abilities. Using norm-referenced test results as the indicator of quality automatically insures certain schools of a high ranking and condemns others to a low ranking, regardless of the educational process used in the schools. Some schools have better "raw material" than others. And, of course, using norm-referenced data is a product approach.

However, if continuous improvement is the criterion, then the fact that a school has an inferior student body based on ability, which usually correlates with socioeconomic data, will not matter in the pursuit of quality. Improvement is possible regardless of the caliber of the raw material, and gives the schools a chance to be recognized positively based on improvement of performance.

The notion of schools using continuous improvement as their measuring stick is reasonable only if the following two assumptions are accepted to begin with:

(1) Given raw material, and the proper equipment, material, training, and time, a product can be turned out that is consistently high in quality.

(2) It is reasonable and feasible to correlate educational standards

with industrial standards in relation to the performance of the operation. In education, the operation is defined as the teaching/learning process.

The acceptance of both of these assumptions is reasonable. But the second assumption contains a condition that holds the key to the educational adaption. This assumption holds that once the operation (educational process) begins, education has the same potential to continuously improve as does industry. However, there is no mention or claim in this assumption concerning the control of the raw material from which the process originates. In the case of industry, the raw material is usually an inanimate object such as metal, mineral, cloth, etc. For schools, the raw material is a human being. Keep in mind that all metals are no more alike than all human beings are alike. The difference lies in the fact that industry can reject metals that do not meet their supplier standards. Therefore, when they begin the operational process, they can be confident that if continuous improvement is not occurring, it is because of something they are doing in the process.

If education is going to do the same, schools must be confident that any breakdowns are in the process, and not due to differences in the raw material (i.e., children) from which the process originated. To do this, schools need to create a situation where the students to whom the control limits are being applied are similar enough that the application of the continuous improvement standard is reasonable. If the school can accomplish this condition, then all the other components of continuous improvement used in industry are reasonable and applicable to education.

To accomplish a condition where the school could say with confidence that all of the students being held to a particular continuous improvement standard are capable of achieving the standard, students will have to be grouped. These groupings are not necessarily the traditional classroom or tracking groups that are normally associated with school grouping patterns. Instead, they would be quality groups. Quality groups are defined by the standards being applied to each individual student with relation to continuous improvement.

This process would not necessarily dictate that all classrooms have only students from one quality group. The term "quality group" refers only to the measurement of continuous improvement. The term means that all members of the quality group are being measured for continuous improvement using the same standard. It is not a physical placement. In other words, it involves saying, "for this student, these standards are reasonable."

What would be the criteria for quality groups? Here are some possibilities:

(1) Students in the college preparatory programs
(2) Ability level as determined by diagnostic testing and assessment
(3) Attendance record
(4) Level of involvement of the students' parents/guardians
(5) Vocational/technical programs

To make this process work, schools would have to accept that once the quality groups were established, any failures that occurred were the result of the process (the educational program) and were not the fault of the raw material (the students). This means that schools would accept the responsibility to work with continuous improvement in human elements such as attitude, attendance, and parental attitude and involvement.

Remember that the standard is continuous improvement, not a fixed norm. Because of all the differences in human beings, and their constant changeability and environmental diversity, fixed standards for all are not reasonable. But continuous improvement is reasonable for every student. It is more than reasonable; it should be expected by both society and the educational community.

The biggest change that schools would have to make to implement the concept of continuous improvement is in the area of statistical analysis. A lot more of the school's resources would have to be allocated to the preservation of, analysis of, distribution of, and attention to student achievement data. The concept can only be accomplished by analyzing student performance, lowering the control limits, and thus working toward continuous improvement.

This reallocation of resources to statistical analysis can be accomplished with no additional administrative costs if schools also adopt the other measures suggested in this chapter. These measures reduce the need for middle management inspection and supervision. Those functions could be replaced by the analysis of and application of statistical testing and assessment data, a function that meets the criterion of being helpful to the operational function of the school. That function is instruction.

Organizational Focus

A school system with organizational focus is one in which the intent, vision, missions, and long-term perspective of the curriculum and instructional program are clear and distinctive. There are time frames on which the system concentrates, which can be adjusted for distinctiveness or clarity. There is a center of interest or activity at which the people of the school system continually and consistently converge. This is defined as the point of focus.

Focus is only effective when it is accompanied by constancy. The problems of today can be solved without constancy, but the problems of tomorrow cannot. For the school that wishes to remain effective and competitive, the problems of both today and tomorrow must form the focus.

The three quality characteristics examined in this chapter are geared to achieving this organizational focus, something that can only be done by looking outside the organization to the people it is meant to serve. These three characteristics are—the use of consumer research, the external quality concept, and quality function deployment. By employing these tools, a school will be able to gain a precise knowledge of its constituents' needs, as well as an understanding of their conception of educational quality. Such needs and wants will define the organizational focus, which will then enable schools to engage in long-term quality planning.

QUALITY CHARACTERISTIC 2—THE USE OF CONSUMER RESEARCH

To use consumer research in education, schools will need to switch their emphasis from information giving to information gathering; they will have to switch from persuasion to perception.

Since successful consumer research is predicated on continual communication, to detect and react to the dynamic and ever-changing world, schools will have to make the organizational changes necessary to accommodate this persistent need.

Since schools have always had a captive audience (attendance areas determined largely by geography) their information sharing has basically involved trying to sell the public on the idea that their program is good and worthy of public support. Therefore, the information has been given to the public in an attempt to persuade them that the school is worth supporting. It has been largely one-way communication. In the cases of two-way communication, the public has usually been asked to react to the school's programs or policies. Seldom have they been asked to initiate programs or policies.

To use consumer research as applied in industry, this mindset would need to change. The school officials would have to rid themselves of the practice of "selling" or "giving," and begin the practice of "gathering." That is, they would have to gather information about what consumers want from the schools in the way of production and services. Public relations would be replaced by consumer research. Most important of all, decisions would be made based on the consumer research.

The key to making consumer research work in schools is identifying the consumer. If the General Motors consumer research division calls up a person and asks, "Do you or have you ever used one of our products?" and the respondent says "No." the interview would be over. It is easy for them to identify their consumers.

It is a little harder for schools. Consumers for schools would best be defined as those who use the school now or who have recently made use of its services. The use could be direct, such as being enrolled as a student or having contact with the school through the use of school facilities, or through contact with the personnel of the school. People with indirect contact could also be defined as consumers. Such people would be parents, grandparents, etc. The characteristic to look for is that the consumer being consulted is basing his/her opinion on direct or indirect contact with the school, and is not relying on second-hand opinion or rumor as the basis of their input. Schools will have to deal with the crackpots. Some subjective judgments about the reactions of consumers would have to accompany the input. In reality, business does not care whether you are a crackpot or not, so long as you buy the product or service. But I think that schools are not going to adopt crackpot ideas just because they are popular, because students could be hurt by such actions. Therefore, consumer research could only drive school decision making to a certain point. While industry only has to ask, "Will it sell?", schools will have to also ask, "Will it hurt students?"

More times than in the private sector, schools will have to reject consumer research. So what? Lots of times it will be used. Consumer research certainly holds more promise than the current state of affairs, which is basically periodic public relations attempts, mostly at tax levy times.

Just as important for schools will be the information gathered that will show what the perceptions are among the clients. Remember, perceptions have replaced persuasion as a goal. These perceptions, if accurate, can be acted upon. If erroneous, the school officials know where their future information giving had better start. That is not the primary purpose of client research, but could be a valuable secondary one.

There are two areas of consumer research used in the private sector that would be hard, if not impossible, to adapt to education. In schools where there is no parental choice, the comparison with other competitive schools would be difficult because the parents would not be knowledgeable about other schools. Secondly, it would be difficult to get the educational community to buy the idea that only local or regional comparison is needed. In areas such as standardized tests, the norming is done on a national basis. Many other accountability ratings are national. However, other areas, such as curriculum, would lend themselves to regional comparative thinking.

Consumer research holds much promise for schools. It would not require more money. It basically calls for a new mindset about how to communicate with the public, which is: first, assume the public has good information for you; second, base decisions on that information; third, switch the emphasis from giving the public information about what you think is important to gathering information about what they think is important, and be open to this public opinion; fourth, move from persuasion to perception; fifth, move from periodic to continual communication with the consumers.

One organizational change would be beneficial. Within the central office, someone will have to be responsible for gathering information, processing information, and presenting that information in such a form that decisions can be made from the data. If you have a public relations person with good communication skills, you've got it made. Just change his/her job function. It doesn't matter which central office person does this function. The point is, it is worth somebody's time. If a priority switch is necessary, make it. The consumers are tired of being told what the schools have done and how great they are. They want the chance to tell you what they think. It works for industry, and it will work for education.

Focus cannot be fully realized unless the school is allowed to be client-driven. Consumer, or client, research is the method that must be employed to achieve a school organization that is client-driven.

A good way to look at consumer research is to examine the process from a series of steps, which, when completed, will produce the information needed to proceed with decision making.

Step 1—Identify the Quality Characteristics That Are Going to Be Used as the Basis for the Research

You should base this selection on topics or areas that the organization has deemed the most important aspects of your operation. You are seeking quality in these areas. Therefore, this is where you want your information.

Some examples of areas which should be the topics of consumer research are:

- curriculum
- programs
- policies
- facilities
- procedures
- services
- personnel

When selecting areas for consumer research, remember to keep in mind the purposes of consumer research:

- to confirm the school's belief in what is good about the school (positive reinforcement)
- to encourage management to combine research with other information in making decisions
- to track data and information for use in compiling statistics over a period of time to verify information such as trends and facts

- to identify problems and successes within the school that no other method or strategy is able to do
- to motivate and reward employees

Step 2—Compile Baseline Data

The importance of baseline data cannot be overemphasized in total quality management. Remember that the standard for total quality management is continuous improvement. The set of baseline data is the starting point from which to begin seeking this continuous improvement.

Step 3—Track Continuously Over a Period of Time

As this data is analyzed, look for trends, tendencies, and variances. The most significant point is that this tracking must be done on an ongoing basis. Otherwise, there is no complete basis upon which to judge continuous improvement.

Step 4—Combine Consumer Research with Other Information/Data and Common Sense in Making Decisions

There are going to be times when decisions cannot be solely based on consumer research. For example, members of your public may indicate that they would like a swimming pool for every building in the district. Common sense, based on cost, will tell you that having a pool in every school is not financially possible.

The point to remember is that consumer research is to be used in conjunction with all the other information and common sense that a school has at its disposal. The key point is that if the school is going to be client-driven, then the wishes of the clients must be taken into account during the decision-making process and not after the fact. Since the school administration cannot call a community meeting every time it wishes to make a decision, the use of ongoing consumer research is a way to include client input during the decision-making process.

In thinking about this process, think in terms of changing current roles, not in terms of adding roles. There is a basic philosophical switch occurring that requires new roles/functions. The switch is from convincing, selling, and informing to gathering information. All schools are currently in the business of the former. That is how tax levies have been passed for generations. Use these same people to begin gathering information.

The training involves six skills:

(1) Constructing written surveys
(2) Synthesizing information
(3) Analyzing information
(4) Presenting the information to divergent groups in a format that can be easily understood
(5) Conducting phone surveys
(6) Identifying the type of client being surveyed

QUALITY CHARACTERISTIC 3—THE EXTERNAL QUALITY CONCEPT

During my research on external quality, I decided that this was one industrial quality characteristic that probably had little or no adaptability to education. It centers on adjusting the relationship with vendors, and exerting more control over their activities. Of course, education has no control over its suppliers or the raw material it accepts. At least the public school doesn't. It must accept whatever comes through the door, ready or not, quality or not.

There are some helpful ideas from the concept, however, that would be valuable to education. First of all, preschool is absolutely essential to improving the incoming students. Secondly, parent training should be a basic component of every school's program. Although schools can't insist on the supplier (parent) coming into the school to learn of the school's expectations, it could offer the opportunity, and would at least improve the quality of the "lot."

External quality lends itself to true partnerships among schools and employers, including higher education. In keeping with the industrial model, school personnel need to go out into the universities and workplaces and find out their needs and expectations. For example, high school teachers need to attend college classes to see what will be expected of their current students when the students reach college. Math and science teachers need to go out into industry and see how their subjects are applied currently in the workplace. Counselors need to visit personnel departments, and administrators need to shadow management. Cross training needs to take place continuously to keep up with the changing nature of the workplace, the future home of the school's product, the student.

The external quality concept is defined as the attempt to improve the quality of the incoming product. In the case of schools, this product is the child or student who is entering school for the first time. Industry works with the vendors who are making the parts which, when assembled will be the finished product.

Schools have two "vendors"—the preschool children, and their parents or guardians. Therefore, schools should have programs for preschool and parenting.

Due to cost, it may be impossible for a school to have preschooling as a part of its ongoing program. If possible, any school wishing to implement the external quality concept should have a preschool program. However, parental training is an absolute necessity.

To continuously improve external quality, schools should consider the child a student from birth. If the school cannot reasonably provide preschool, then regular training for the parents/guardians is a must. This training should have a twofold purpose—development of parenting skills for parents, and basic skill development for the child.

The school can only achieve external quality by going out and working with the preschool parent. This could be done by hiring an additional kindergarten teacher, so that one kindergarten teacher at a time could be released to work with the parenting program. If there are other personnel who could be redirected to participate in this program, that would be desirable.

Treat Textbook Companies as Vendors

The current relationship between textbook publishers and schools is neither effective nor efficient. Textbook publishers write books, market them, and sell them to schools. This publishing approach assumes that a national curriculum is in existence. That, of course, is not true. Therefore, the marketing strategy of textbook publishers is flawed.

Schools need to work more closely with textbook publishers during the writing process. By doing so, frontloading of the curriculum would be feasible.

The key to achieving external quality with textbook publishers is through the curriculum development process. Theoretically, this process should work as follows:

(1) Schools should develop the curriculum.
(2) Schools should choose a textbook that correlates in scope and sequence with the curriculum.

This two-step process is known as frontloading. It is the ideal, theoretically sound way to correlate curriculum and textbooks.

The problem is that there are thousands of school districts in the United States, but only a handful of textbook publishers. That means that there are thousands of curriculum developments occurring, with variations. Therefore, the correlation between curriculum and textbooks is very difficult.

As a result of this problem, backloading is more prevalent than frontloading in curriculum. Backloading is a two-step process that is the opposite of frontloading. Backloading is:

(1) Schools select a textbook.
(2) Schools develop the curriculum to correlate with the textbook.

The problem with this approach is that the curriculum of the school is being driven by textbook publishers. That would be okay if there was communication between the school and the publishers during the process. In other words, if the school had input. If this was occurring, then the external quality concept would be in operation. But because of marketing realities and publishing costs, textbook publishers do not produce books for a school system.

But could they? Yes, if it was profitable for them. In order for the external quality concept to occur between schools and their most significant vendors, textbook publishers, schools must begin looking at the curriculum development process as a consortium. This consortium must be large enough to attract a publisher. The criterion for this attraction is simply that the consortium will produce a market large enough for the publisher to turn a profit.

Curriculum consortiums are only feasible as long as the participating schools are philosophically compatible. They must all be in agreement as to the content and format approach to the subject. For example, schools using the whole language approach to language arts would be a feasible consortium. A school using a traditional grammar approach with basal texts would not be a good partner in the whole language curriculum consortium.

A curriculum consortium could be as large as a state, or a region within a state. The only criteria are that there is philosophical congruence among the participating schools and a large enough membership to make the venture profitable for the publisher. When these two elements are present, the schools can form a long-term relationship with the vendor, then the vendor and the schools can come to understand each other's needs and limits, and the external quality concept can be achieved.

During this process, the publishing companies would send their writers and editors to work in the schools to get an idea of how the schools intended to use their books. The schools would send teachers to the publishing companies to assist their writers and editors in developing the content for the texts. That is the external quality concept in action.

The long-term relationship is vital. That is how industry has improved its quality. Industries no longer use the lowest bidder and they no longer bid all vendor contracts every year. They look for long-term relationships with one or a few vendors and work together toward quality, i.e., the external quality concept. By using the long-term relationship, textbook publishers would be willing to work with smaller consortiums. They would sacrifice larger short-term profits for long-term stability with smaller profits.

For quality to improve in schools, there needs to be a much stronger connection between curriculum and textbooks (learning materials). Schools and textbook publishers should derive curriculum content and the textbook content simultaneously.

Noneducational Material Vendors

Schools purchase from vendors in the areas of food, maintenance supplies and equipment, transportation supplies and equipment, and other noninstructional areas. Cooperative bidding on a yearly basis is a common practice for schools. The contracts are released to the lowest bidder. This is not external quality in action. The schools should attempt to find a few vendors willing to work on a long-term basis with the schools to improve quality.

One area in which the benefits of this long-term relationship can be illustrated is in the printing area. Criterion-referenced testing material and brochures explaining programs require tedious printing, collation, and dissemination of details. A long-term relationship with one vendor will reduce the amount of time and resources needed to instruct the vendor each year. If you change vendors every year, these details have to be gone over, which requires continual use of time, a valuable resource. In the long run, a school will get better quality and save money and resources by using the external quality concept, with fewer vendors and more long-term relationships with them.

QUALITY CHARACTERISTIC 4—QUALITY FUNCTION DEPLOYMENT

Currently, the power of the school decision-making structure lies within the formal organization of the school. That is, the board of education, the administration, and the teachers' union are the primary decision makers. Community input is solicited, but mostly on an advisory basis.

In order for schools to use quality function deployment, more educational decisions (curriculum, instruction, testing) will have to be made by the clients of the school. The clients of the school are the students, parents/guardians, and the other affected populations of the community.

Quality function deployment is the shifting of the power in the drive for quality from the institution itself to the clients of the institution. Therefore, this point involves the board of education, the administration, and the teachers' union because they are the current power structures in schools.

Therefore, the school wishing to pursue quality function deployment must ask itself the following questions:

(1) Are the board, the administration, and the union as currently functioning practicing quality function deployment?

(2) Is the quality function deployment properly balanced among the clients of the school?

If the current quality power structure can answer both of these questions with a yes, then the quality function deployment concept is in place. If not, the following steps should be taken: (1) utilize consumer research and other input/feedback gathering techniques to create quality function deployment; (2) identify school clients beyond students, parents/guardians, future employers, and higher education institutions, i.e., special interest groups, or particular economic, social, or religious groups; and (3) identify their chief interests.

Quality function deployment would require the board, the administration, and the teachers' union to give up power. The board members must accept the philosophical stance that even though they were elected by the public to represent them in decision making, the ongoing input of the public is required and desired, and will be followed. The administration must accept educational direction from their clients even though many of them are not professional educators. And the teachers' union must accept responsibility for more than their own employment interests and devote more time to the interests of the institution, and therefore the clients.

Most important of all, these groups will have to commit themselves to sticking with quality function deployment and indeed with the whole total quality management movement for the long term. One of the most harmful of current trends in both American industry and American education is the emphasis on short-term results rather than long-term planning and transformation.

The total quality movement in the United States resulted from the observation that the major difference between management here and in Japan was that American businesses generally took the short-term view (being driven by quarterly profits or losses) while the Japanese took the long-term view (staying in business, providing jobs).

The problems that American schools face are different from those of business, but they are just as acute. Schools didn't get into their present condition in a short time, and they can't change in a short time. It will require long-term thinking to provide long-term solutions. That long-term thinking must have a sufficient time frame to allow the system to establish itself, and begin to produce results. Without such a commitment, the organizational focus will simply shift from year to year as the winds of politics blow, making it impossible to achieve quality of any sort.

Measuring Progress in Schools

Once a school commits itself to constant improvement and achieves a workable organizational focus, the question naturally arises as to how this constant improvement will be measured. The quality characteristics discussed in this chapter attempt to answer that question. They are—statistical process control, the internal quality concept, and the use of human sensors. Using these tools, it will be possible to determine what a school can improve, and what it should not even try to improve. It is important to remember throughout this discussion that schools primarily involve people, not machines, so any measurements will by nature be less precise than those employed by heavy industry.

QUALITY CHARACTERISTIC 5—STATISTICAL PROCESS CONTROL

Statistical process control (SPC) means that the students and teachers of the school are doing the best that they can under the existing educational processes of the school. In order for this to occur, the educational processes of the school must be in a state of stability. This state of stability would mean that the school is operating in such a way that the maximum potential for teachers (teaching) and students (learning) is feasible.

Statistical process control concentrates on the learning process, not on individual achievement data. Individual achievement data is determined by many variables, some of which the school has little or no control over. Therefore, for the school to attempt to exercise statistical control over these variables is counterproductive. However, the school can exercise influence over the learning processes that are practiced by the schools. It is in this realm that statistical process control concentrates.

The specific purposes for SPC in schools are: (1) to explain variation through the proper use of special and common causes; (2) to use statistical data to make predictions, and thus proactively affect educational decision making; and (3) to provide data to answer the question, "How are we doing?"

The role of leadership in SPC is to identify and take care of special causes and improve the system. Statistical process control is not another name for personnel appraisal. SPC works to improve the overall system of educational processes at work in the school. Variation in individuals, both students and teachers, is a natural phenomenon. The best way to work with this natural variation is through maximizing the educational processes so that everyone can work to his/her capacity.

Statistical process control tools, such as charts, should all relate to organizational aims and should measure criteria on a consistent basis. Their purpose is not to rank, but to improve the educational processes. Statistical process control should have as its goal the continuous improvement of the school, and should work with control limits, not specification limits. (This will be explained in detail in the discussion of the quality point "applying statistical process improvement tools.")

Because of the nature of public education, equity is an issue in statistical process control. It is the aim of public education to educate all the population, regardless of the variations that occur in ability, motivation, environment, and state of readiness. Therefore, in assessing the stability of educational processes, the school must add the additional component of equitability for all clients.

Applying Statistical Process Improvement Tools

Statistical process improvement tools are used for system analysis. Specifically, their purpose is to identify special causes and react to them. Also, the tools are to help with predictability, which allows leadership to be proactive in the decision-making process.

Following are a group of statistical tools that could be used for SPC in the attempt to continuously improve the quality of the educational processes of the school. This is not intended to be a cookbook. Each school should base its use of tools on its own aims. If these aims vary from school to school, the tools used will most likely vary also. It will depend on what educational processes are the most important to the school. The following statistical tools assume that the most important educational processes are (1) curriculum, (2) instruction, (3) correlation between curriculum and assessment, (4) congruity between curriculum and instruction, (5) attendance of staff and students, (6) number of student dropouts, (7) educational environment, and (8) utilization of resources.

Pareto Charts

This chart derives its name from the Pareto Principle, which states that 80 percent of the trouble comes from 20 percent of the problems. Pareto charts enable management to concentrate on the "vital few" and ignore the "trivial many." Therefore, its purpose is to focus improvement efforts by ranking problems or their causes.

A Pareto chart is a series of bars whose heights reflect the frequency or impact of problems. The bars are arranged in descending order of height from left to right. This means the categories represented by the tall bars on the left are relatively more important than those on the right.

Pareto charts are useful throughout the improvement process. Early on, they identify which problems should be studied, and later they narrow down which causes of the problem to address first. They dramatically and clearly draw attention to the "vital few."

There are two types of Pareto charts. A Pareto chart by phenomena is a diagram concerning the undesirable results in quality, cost, or delivery system, and is used to find the identity of the major problem. A Pareto chart by causes is a diagram concerning causes in the process, and is used to find out the major cause of the problem.

Pareto Chart by Phenomena

The following chart (Figure 6.1) shows student failures in a high school by subject areas for a school year. The chart reveals that ninety-five students failed an English class. Ninety students failed a math class. No other subject areas had more than thirty incidents of student failure. This chart focuses, therefore, on the major problem—failures in English and math. These two subject areas are the "vital few." All the other subject bars represent the "trivial many." This is not to suggest

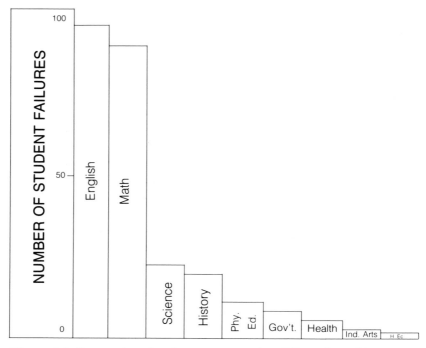

Figure 6.1 *Pareto chart by phenomena—student failures by subject areas.*

88

that any student failure is not significant or important. But remember that we are trying to apply SPC to the educational system. From that perspective, the system's problem with student failures lies in English and math. It could even be assumed that the failure rates in the other subject areas are due to common cause, and, therefore, cannot be tampered with unless there is a complete change in the system.

This chart has only identified the problem. A second analysis is needed to begin to address the problem.

Pareto Chart by Causes

This chart (Figure 6.2) represents the school's study of why students are failing English. The chart reveals that thirty students failed due to poor composition quality. Thirty students failed due to inadequate reading levels. These two bars are the "vital few." The other bars represent poor test scores, not handing in assignments, lack of participation, and other causes. These are the "trivial many."

This chart tells the school that if officials and teachers concentrate their improvement efforts on correcting composition skills and improving reading levels, they will have the best chance to reduce student failures in English.

An Ineffective Pareto Chart

To be effective, a Pareto chart must provide specific data about a specific problem. Figure 6.3 represents an ineffective Pareto chart because the "other" bar (which is a "vital few" bar) is not specific enough to initiate corrective action. "Other" could mean anything. Therefore, the school must find out what those "others" are before the analysis of the problem has any corrective potential.

Cause and Effect Diagrams

Cause and effect diagrams are used to identify and organize possible causes of problems, or factors needed to insure success in some effort or process. The result of a process can be attributed to a multitude of factors, and a cause and effect relation can be found among those factors. We can determine the structure or a multiple cause and effect relationship by observing it systematically. It is difficult to solve compli-

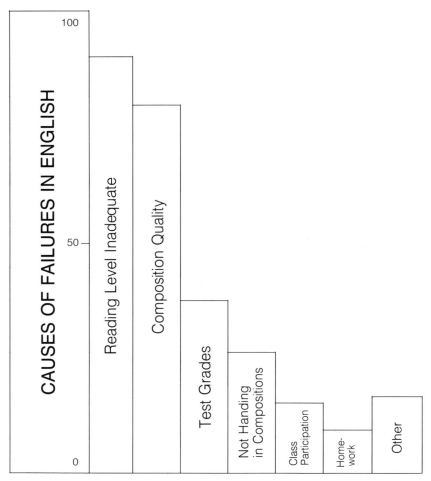

Figure 6.2 Pareto chart by causes — causes of student failures in English.

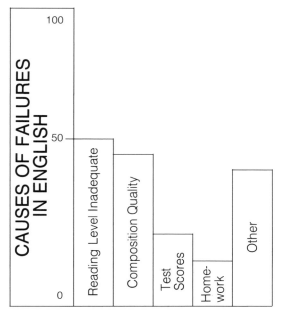

Figure 6.3 *Ineffective Pareto chart — other bar too large.*

cated problems without considering the structure. Any structure consists of a chain of causes and effects. Therefore, a cause and effect diagram is a method of expressing a problem simply and easily.

The cause and effect diagram is a diagram that shows the relationship between a quality characteristic and contributing factors. It is also called a "fishbone diagram" because of its appearance. This type of diagram was invented by Kaoru Ishikawa, and is hence also called an Ishikawa diagram. It has proven to be an effective tool for studying processes and situations, and for planning.

The procedure for making cause and effect diagrams for identifying causes is illustrated in Figure 6.4, and goes as follows:

(1) Determine the quality characteristic effect (low student motivation/interest in history classes).

(2) Choose one quality characteristic (effect) and write it in the big square on the right hand side of the paper (low student motivation/interest in history classes).

(3) Write the primary factors that affect the quality characteristic as

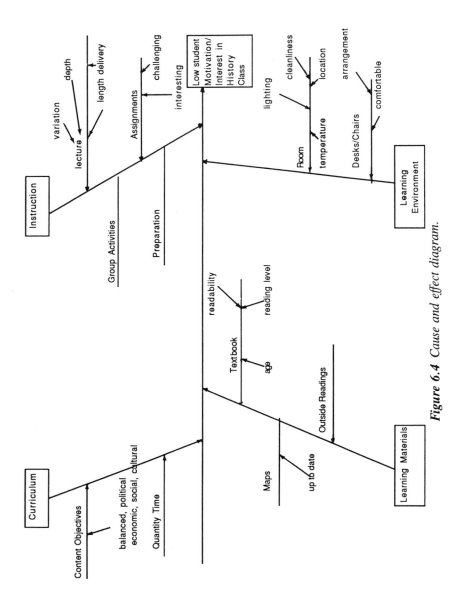

Figure 6.4 Cause and effect diagram.

big bones also enclosed by a square (curriculum, instruction, learning/teaching materials, learning environment).

(4) Write the causes (secondary causes) that affect the big bones (primary causes) as medium-sized bones, and write the causes (tertiary causes) that affect the medium-sized bones as small bones.

(5) Assign an importance to each factor, and mark particularly important factors that seem to have a significant effect on the quality characteristic.

(6) Record any necessary information.

Arranging causes and effects in this manner will lead to a greater understanding of the problem and possible contributing factors. The diagram should then serve as a basis for a detailed discussion of how the process works, and how the cause and effect relations function. Then the significance of the various "bones" can be determined and action planned. The key to making the cause and effect diagram work is to assign the significance (importance) of each factor identified on the diagram objectively on the basis of data.

Examination of factors on the basis of your own skill and experience is important, but it is dangerous to give importance to them through subjective perceptions and impressions alone. If the problem could be solved by this approach, it probably would already have been solved. Assigning importance to factors objectively using data is both more scientific and more logical.

Scatter Diagrams

The scatter diagram allows you to look at the relationship between two characteristics, something that is often essential in education. The shape of the resulting scatter of points tells you if the two factors are related. If they are unrelated, the points will be randomly scattered around the graph. If larger values of one occur with larger values of the other, the points will group toward a line running from lower left to upper right. If larger values of one are associated with smaller values of the other, the points will cluster on a line running from upper left to lower right.

The following scatter diagrams show the relationship between the number of handicapped students infused into a regular classroom and the number of disciplinary referrals from that classroom (see Figure 6.5).

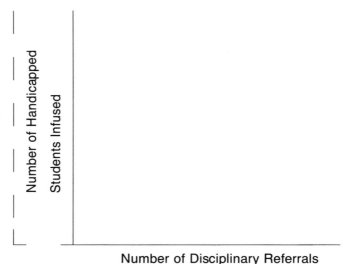

Figure 6.5 *Scatter diagram.*

Figure 6.6 shows a positive correlation between the two processes. In other words, the more that handicapped students were infused into the classroom, the more disciplinary referrals were made.

Figure 6.7 shows a negative correlation between the two processes.

Figure 6.8 indicates that there may be a positive correlation present, while Figure 6.9 indicates that a negative correlation may be present. Figures 6.10 and 6.11 clearly indicate no correlation between the two processes.

It is clear how the data of a scatter diagram could be used, but this is only a first step. Let's assume that it showed a positive correlation in the example we used. The fact that disciplinary referrals increased suggests a problem. But we do not yet know the specifics of that problem. Are the disciplinary actions all occurring with the handicapped students? Have the number of disciplinary referrals among the regular students increased? If so, is it related to the infusion process? All these are questions that would have to be answered before the problem could be approached. However, what the scatter diagram showed was that the problem exists and that it is somehow connected to the relationship between the two processes.

What if no correlation was shown to exist but the regular classroom teacher insisted that the infusion process had increased disciplinary

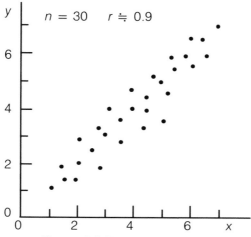

Figure 6.6 *Positive correlation.*

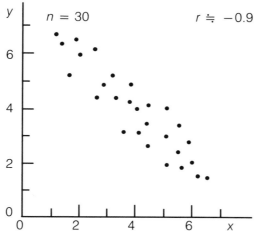

Figure 6.7 *Negative correlation.*

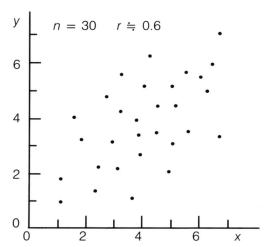

Figure 6.8 *Positive correlation may be present.*

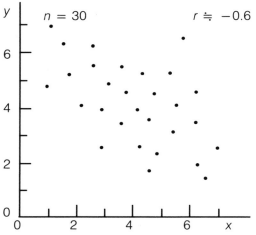

Figure 6.9 *Negative correlation may be present.*

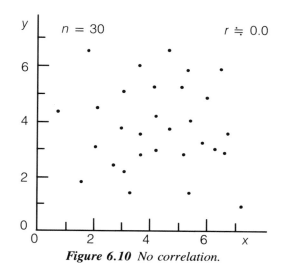

Figure 6.10 No correlation.

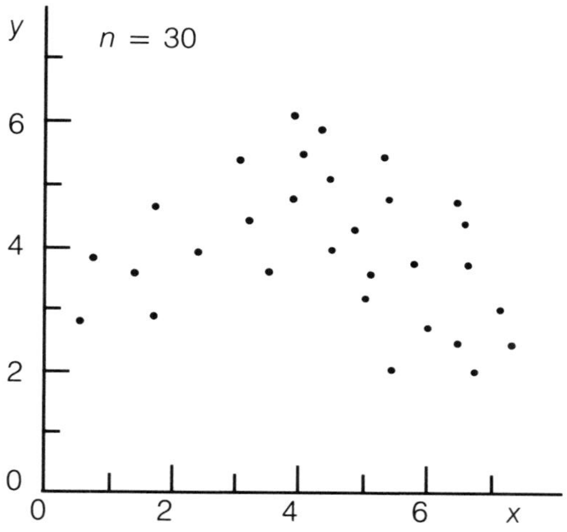

y | $n = 30$ | $r \doteqdot 0.0$

Figure 6.11 No correlation.

y | $n = 30$

referrals? The scatter diagram would provide data to show that such an assumption was incorrect. Therefore, no further time and resources would be used on a nonexisting problem. That is the purpose of SPC—to use data to govern leadership and decision making.

Figure 6.12 is another scatter diagram that shows a positive correlation between the number of courses a student fails and the decision of that student to drop out of school. This is another example of a school trying to isolate the causes of quality problems so that leadership can be given to the solution of the problems as identified by data, not supposition.

Control Charts

Control charts are used to monitor a process to see whether or not it is in statistical control. The upper control limits (UCL) and the lower control limits (LCL) indicate how much variation is typical of the process. Points that fall outside the limits or into particular patterns indicate the presence of a special cause of variation, a cause that deserves investigation.

Control Chart for Curriculum/Instruction

Figure 6.13 is a control chart to monitor the Algebra I curriculum. Horizontally, the chart represents a school year, divided up into four quarters. The planned curriculum objectives are represented by x. The upper control limits represent a 10 percent increase in objectives taught, while the lower control limits represent a 10 percent decrease in objectives taught. This curriculum process is stable according to the control chart. No points are outside the upper or lower control limits. The variation that is occurring is due to normal variation in the ability and motivation of the students. To tinker with the process in any way is fruitless. Teachers who are near the lower control limits should not be told to "speed it up." Teachers near the upper control limits should not be told to "slow down." Common causes are at work. The process is stable.

Figure 6.14 shows a control chart that indicates a process out of control. Many of the points are outside the control limits. Three of the Algebra I classes have exceeded the curriculum plan by 40 percent. One of the Algebra I classes has not covered 30 percent of the planned

NUMBER OF COURSES FAILED

y

x

Figure 6.12 Dropout decision.

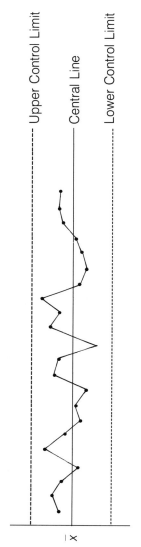

Figure 6.13 *Control chart for controlled state.*

100

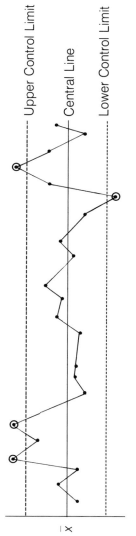

Figure 6.14 *Control chart for out-of-control state.*

curriculum. This means that some special causes are at work, and they need to be investigated.

How to Read Control Charts

What is most important in process control is to grasp the state of process accurately by reading a control chart, and to take appropriate action promptly when anything unusual in the process is found. The controlled state of a process is the state in which the process is stable and the process average and variation do not change. Whether a process is in the controlled state or not is judged by the following criteria from the control chart.

(1) *Out of Control Limits*. Points are outside of the control limits (Figure 6.14).

(2) *Run*. Run is a state in which points occur continually on one side of the central line ($\bar{x}$). The number of points is called the length of the run. Figure 6.15 shows a run above the central line. This chart indicates that the curriculum plan does not contain sufficient objectives and should be augmented with additional content.

Figure 6.15 also shows a run below the central line, which indicates that the curriculum plan contains too many objectives and, therefore, some of the content needs to be deleted.

Keep in mind that adding or deleting learning objectives involves changing the process. When that is done, a new control chart needs to be constructed and used. Even though in both of these instances the process was in statistical control, the presence of the runs indicated an opportunity for improvement by changing the process or system. If this fundamental change was not going to be made, then the existing system, which was producing the run, should not be tampered with. To do so would only cause chaos and frustration.

(3) *Trend*. When the points form a continuous upward or downward curve, the process is said to have a trend. Figure 6.16 shows both an upward and downward trend. An upward trend would indicate that more Algebra I classes are finishing the learning objectives faster. A downward trend would indicate that more Algebra I classes are having difficulty finishing the curriculum objectives on time.

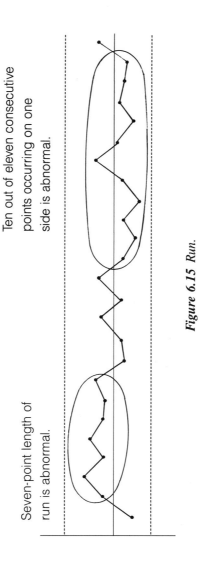

Figure 6.15 Run.

When the points form a continuous upward or downward curve, this is said to have a trend.

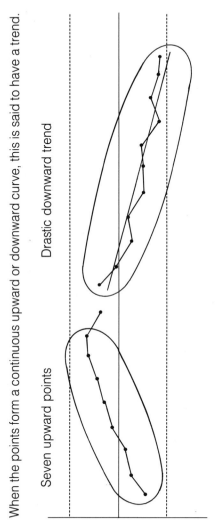

Seven upward points

Drastic downward trend

Figure 6.16 Trend.

The school wishing to be proactive and use predictability to lead will use this data to adjust the process before it becomes out of control.

(4) *Approach to the Control Limits.* If two out of three points occur near the outside control limits (either upper or lower) the process is considered to be abnormal and in need of attention. Figure 6.17 shows this situation.

Control Chart on Teacher Absenteeism

Figure 6.18 shows a time plot for teacher absenteeism for an entire school year. However, the chart does not create a basis for decision making or problem solving. It does show time-related shifts, trends, and patterns that could serve as valuable data to plan improvement.

Based on this data plus other objective, scientific information, control limits could be set, and a control chart instituted for teacher absenteeism (see Figure 6.19). With the control chart, the school could decide on an ongoing basis when teacher absenteeism was following common causes, and thus was not treatable, and when it was due to a special cause, and thus was treatable.

Prerequisite to Quality Control of Curriculum/Instruction/Testing

Figure 6.20 shows a quality control triangle for education.[19] This triangle is easy to achieve with criterion-referenced testing as the type of assessment being used. However, with the political reality of today, it is difficult for a school to use only criterion- or curriculum-referenced testing. Communities are demanding to know how the local school compares to other schools in the area, state, and nation. Even international comparison is now sometimes demanded. Therefore, norm-referenced tests are required in order to make the comparisons.

To use the quality control triangle found in Figure 6.20 without knowing if the testing component is measuring the other two points of the triangle (namely curriculum and instruction) will not produce quality control of the educational process. Therefore, the first step in applying the quality triangle is to analyze the standardized test being used to

[19]English, F. 1988. *Curriculum Auditing.* Lancaster, PA: Technomic Publishing Co., Inc., p. 111.

Considering points which approach the 3-sigma control limits, if two out of three points occur outside of the 2-sigma lines, this case is considered to be abnormal.

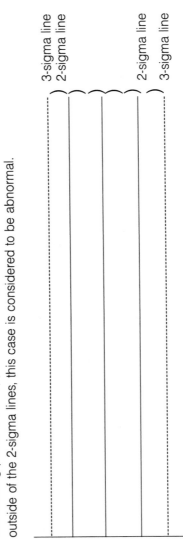

Figure 6.17 Approach to the Control Limits (two out of three points).

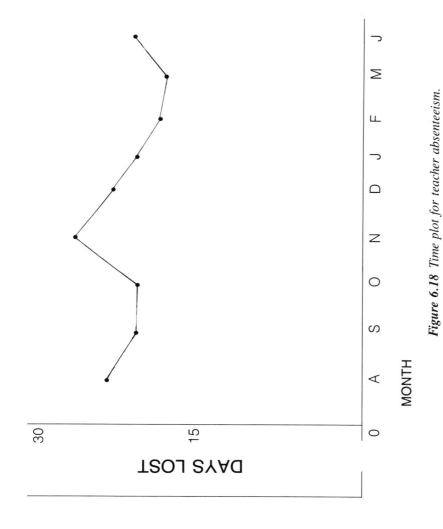

Figure 6.18 Time plot for teacher absenteeism.

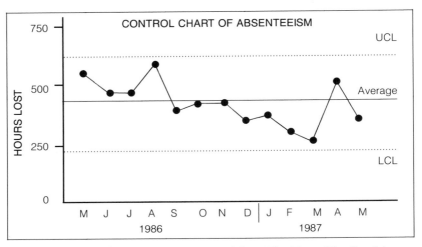

Figure 6.19 *Control chart (reprinted from* The Team Handbook*).*

insure that it is truly measuring the curriculum and, thus, the instruction.

Figure 6.21 shows a standardized test study by a school system.[20] Notice that the school studied four testing companies by determining the "match" between the tests and the curriculum. This particular aspect of the study centered in language arts. Notice that none of the testing companies presented a total (100 percent) match. However, companies A and B were a better match than companies C and D. It is logical to assume that the school can easily narrow the selection down to two testing companies, A and B.

The percentage difference between A and B are minute. Therefore, some other consideration could be used to determine which test best measures the school curriculum. Figure 6.22,[20] showing another component of the analysis of the testing companies, reveals the format of the tests. Notice that companies A and B have organized the test similarly with one exception. Company B assesses listening skills, which company A does not. This could be a reason to choose company B, since there was no significant difference in the curriculum match.

[20]Martin, C. Unpublished manuscript, Clermont Co. Board of Education, Batavia, OH, 1990.

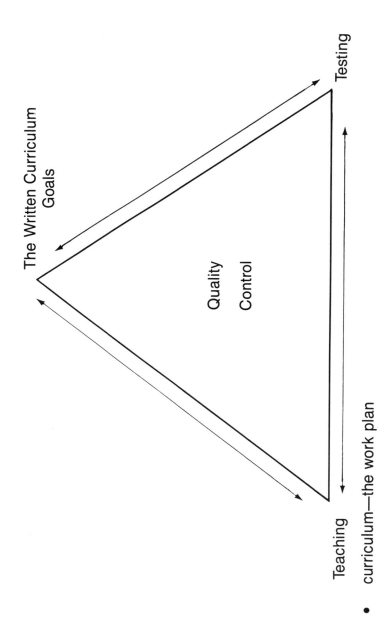

Figure 6.20 The curriculum audit – basic construct for auditing rational systems.

The Written Curriculum
Goals

Testing

Quality
Control

Teaching

- curriculum—the work plan
- teaching—the work
- testing—work measurement

Test Company	A	B	C	D
Test Title	A	B	C	D
Curriculum match to language arts graded course of study, 1988 edition, by percent at grades				
4	84%	82%	78%	64%
6	94%	93%	84%	87%
8	93%	96%	87%	88%
10 Basic	84%	87%	79%	77%
10 General	92%	93%	85%	90%
10 College prep./honors	94%	93%	87%	90%

Figure 6.21 *Standardized testing study—language arts (reading and English).*

Notice that company D (see Figure 6.22) has only four testing sections. This is pointed out to illustrate that all standardized tests are not alike.

After choosing the testing company, the school then has a second decision to make. Assuming that testing company B was selected, this means that 91 percent of the curriculum of the school (all grades tested combined) will be assessed. Is that good enough? I don't think so; not if you are truly interested in total quality. According to classical quality control models, the school can take one or more of the following steps: (1) Revise the curriculum so that 100 percent of the curriculum is tested. This means dropping 9 percent of the curriculum. (2) Through an item analysis, determine which aspects of the curriculum are not being tested, and view the testing results from this revised perspective; in other words, disregard the testing results in the areas that are not covered by the curriculum. (3) Revise the curriculum so that 100 percent of the test is covered by the curriculum. This would mean adding those objectives that were assessed by the standardized test and were not a part of the current curriculum. Any of these three methods would create the "match" needed between curriculum and testing to confidently say that quality control measures were in place.

	A	B	C	D
Test Company	A	B	C	D
Test Title	A	B	C	D
Curriculum match to language arts graded course of study, 1988 edition, by percent at grade Test Sections	93% Vocabulary Comprehension Spelling Language Mechanics Language Expression Study Skills	96% Reading Vocabulary Reading Comprehension Spelling Language Mechanics Language Expression Study Skills Listening Skills	87% Vocabulary Reading Comprehension Spelling Capitalization Punctuation Usage & Expression Visual Materials Reference Materials	88% Vocabulary Reading Comprehension Mechanics of Writing English Expression

Figure 6.22 Standardized testing study—language arts (reading and English).

From the total quality perspective, however, all three of these procedures are undesirable. Using both procedures one and three is tantamount to letting the testing company decide what the curriculum should be. Procedure two would be very difficult to do. All testing printout analyses are based on the total battery of the test. To attempt to disregard some of the data would render the testing analysis information useless. Therefore, the school would have to do its own item analysis, which would be difficult. Such a decision would also make the test percentiles, stanines, means, medians, and modes nonusable.

Testing companies are vendors for the schools. However, currently the vendors (testing companies) are making the decisions about the process and the product for the companies (the schools). In other words, education has the process backwards. Testing companies are deciding what content should be tested, and how it should be tested. Schools are then altering their educational process (curriculum and instruction) to accommodate the vendor.

If education is serious about statistical process control, this process must be reversed. Schools must begin deciding what and how to test, and then contract with vendors to supply that service. Education and testing should be a partnership, similar to what manufacturing companies have with their suppliers. Each must understand the needs and limitations of the other. Certainly, testing companies have expertise that schools don't always have, and schools have expertise that testing companies don't have. It is obvious that they should not be working in isolation from each other, as they are currently doing.

If this so obvious, why does it continue? The answer is economics. Testing companies, under the current thinking paradigms, will not devise tests tailored to each individual school. The market isn't big enough to make it profitable. Therefore, schools must organize their curriculum in such a way as to make it profitable for the testing companies. How?

There is more than one way. One way is to combine schools into a regional or state curriculum center that could identify the scope and sequence of the curriculum, and contract testing based on the content. The testing/curriculum consortium should only include schools whose philosophical beliefs are in agreement. Schools should form partnerships based on philosophy, not geography.

When this partnership becomes a large enough market, it should then negotiate with a testing company for a total testing package.

A second strategy is for the educational community to insist that testing companies work from a new perspective. That perspective is one of test item banks. These item banks could be developed mutually among testing companies and school districts to insure that there were test items for all school curricula. Then each school would select the 100 percent match between its curriculum and the test items. Ridiculous, you say? Not with total quality thinking. One of the driving forces behind the total quality movement is the new relationship between companies and their vendors. For education to attain SPC, schools must gain more input into two areas—textbook content and standardized testing content.

To continue to teach and test without absolute knowledge that these two processes are correlated totally renders the notion of SPC impossible. Many critics of the quality approach to education use the fact that education is a variable process as a reason that it can't be measured. The old rationale says that to compare schools is to compare "apples with oranges." That rationale is supported by the current state of affairs in testing. But it would not hold true if a school knew what it was teaching and testing. With knowledge and input into all three points of the quality triangle (curriculum, instruction, and testing) statistical process control is feasible for schools.

Using Control Charts for Continuous Improvement

Figure 6.23 illustrates a flow diagram for making a control chart.[21] Please refer to the far right hand column that refers to the fact that the school system may decide, based on data, that significant improvement is feasible. In that case, some change in the educational process would be made, and a new control chart would be made. Figure 6.24 illustrates this process in operation.

The significant aspects of SPC are that the school is working toward continuous improvement. This continuous improvement is pursued through working with the educational processes using the process improvement tools described in this chapter. Alterations in any process will be based on data, and new control limits will reflect what experience has shown about performance. In this way there is no guesswork and no tinkering with stable systems.

---

[21]Deming, W. E. 1991. *Quality, Productivity and Competitive Position*. Los Angeles, CA: Quality Enhancement Seminars, Inc., p. 12.

Decide what quality characteristic to plot. Decide what kind of chart might be helpful. Decide on plan for collection of data. Decide scales for format of chart. Achieve statistical control of system of measurement.

Start chart. Consider revision of plan. Decide whether to continue the chart, or to revise the plan.

Work on special cause indicated by a point out of control.

With good luck, reach statistical control.

Work on some definite change in the process for improvement (less variation, different level). Consideration of economics may lead to a decision not to make any change at this time, in which case, drop the chart, restore it from time to time to learn whether statistical control continues.

Responsibility of engineers and of people close to the job. The operator will usually plot the job and work on identification and removal of special causes.

Responsibility of management.

Figure 6.23 Flow diagram for making a control chart.

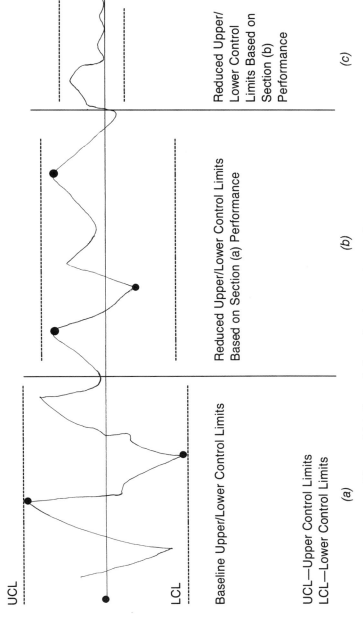

Figure 6.24 Control chart showing continuous improvement process.

UCL

LCL

Baseline Upper/Lower Control Limits

(a)

Reduced Upper/Lower Control Limits
Based on Section (a) Performance

(b)

Reduced Upper/
Lower Control
Limits Based on
Section (b)
Performance

(c)

UCL—Upper Control Limits
LCL—Lower Control Limits

115

Common/Special Causes

Some understanding of variation, including appreciation of a stable system, and some understanding of special causes and common causes of variation, is essential for management of a system, including the management of people.

This quality point is pursued in order to assess the stability of the educational processes of the school. When the data indicates that a process is stable, that means that the distribution of the output of the process is predictable. In other words, the process is in a state of statistical control. Once a process has been brought into a state of statistical control, it has a definable capacity. A process that is not in statistical control does not have a definable capacity, i.e., its performance is not predictable.

In order to know if a process is in a state of statistical control, one must understand the differences between common and special causes. Dr. Shewhart invented a way to think about the differences in variation, which involved avoiding two major mistakes:

(1) To attribute to a special cause a problem when in fact the problem came from common causes of variation
(2) To attribute to common causes of variation a problem when in fact the problem came from a special cause of variation

A school system will be effective with control charts only if its members are adept at identifying common and special causes. Without this knowledge, the school will never be sure when a process is in statistical control, and therefore will not be able to work with continuous improvement.

QUALITY CHARACTERISTIC 6—THE INTERNAL QUALITY CONCEPT

To apply internal quality concepts, education must first identify who are its internal customers. Basically, the internal customers in schools are the people who make up the vertical school organizational structure. Internal customers for preschools are primary schools, for primary schools they are intermediate schools, for intermediate schools they are middle schools, for middle schools they are high schools, and for high schools they are colleges and the world of work (employers).

Then, educational planning must be totally integrated, preschool through adulthood. No longer should a primary school plan educational programming without at least preschool and intermediate personnel being a part.

That in itself is not new. Education has been saying that for decades. However, the basic premise underlying this integrated dialogue might be different. When preschool education is being planned, the starting point must be to ask the primary school, "What are your needs?" The starting point for primary school planning must be to ask the intermediate school, "What are your needs?" and so forth and so on up the ladder to the adult world.

This process should start with high schools asking colleges and employers, "What are your needs, now and in the foreseeable future?" From here, the process should work downward all the way to preschool. That is not happening in schools today. Planning is much more segregated and individual. When the various levels of education plan, they begin by asking, "What are our needs?" or "What should we teach?" The needs of internal customers are given very little consideration.

Taking into account the needs of internal customers would change schooling. It would create an automatic partnership among schools, higher education, and employers. This partnership would be ongoing, legitimate, institutionalized, and integrated.

Education cannot implement this concept of internal quality until people in the various levels learn enough about each other to intelligently ask the question, "What are your needs?" and be able to respond. Therefore, a program of staff development that would raise the level of awareness of all of the educational community about the entire educational spectrum, preschool to employment as an adult, would be the first step toward internal quality.

Internal quality in the schools would be better served if the school could cut down on the number of different operations performed on each student. For example, teachers would stay with students for more than one year in the elementary grades. And, in keeping with the industrial model, teachers would work in teams to validate internal quality by adjusting curriculum and instruction to meet student needs.

Would this be worth it to schools? There would have to be a lot of changes to make the industrial concept of internal quality fit education. For example, teacher preparation might have to change from specific certification such as elementary, to more general certification such as kindergarten through grade twelve. In this way, all teaching levels would have knowledge of all the rest, and integrated planning would be far easier.

The term *internal quality* does not mean that this process is restricted to the schools themselves. If the concept is taken in its total industrial definition, then employers and higher education are involved in the process. It would not be difficult to include them. For example, a senior course could be "job skills and attitudes." A senior would have to spend two weeks in a job and receive a passing grade from the company. Any student who refuses or fails would not receive the work readiness guarantee. Any who completed the job satisfactorily would receive the guarantee.

QUALITY CHARACTERISTIC 7—THE USE OF HUMAN SENSORS

The weakness of human sensors has long been central to many educators' arguments that schools can't use the industrial quality model. The reasoning has always been that all of education, even testing, involves human sensing. Education has also assumed that all of industry's quality measurements were done with gauges or other scientific devices. Neither of these scenarios is accurate. Currently, industry is pursuing a quality model that assumes that people, not machines, make and measure quality. In that sense, they are moving closer to what education has assumed for a long time.

It is true that many of industry's products can be specified and controlled by gauges, tools, or other mechanical, electrical, or chemical devices. In those cases, human sensing is not vital to the maintenance of quality standards. Of course, education only has one product—a human being and the knowledge, skills, and attitudes that are developed as a result of his/her schooling experience. So the opportunity to avoid human sensing is never present in education. Therefore, the study of the design and use of devices—mechanical, electrical, or chemical—to maintain quality has no use in the pursuit of educational excellence.

However, one of the most interesting aspects of the research on current industrial quality efforts is that the exclusive use of nonhuman devices is not sufficient to maintain competitive quality. That is because continuous improvement has replaced specific tolerances as the measuring stick for quality. A gauge can measure the degree of conformance to a specified tolerance, but the pursuit of continuous improvement must involve the use of the human mind, and thus human sensing. Quality today involves the continuous effort to improve the product. If the specified tolerance for a spindle is plus or minus .005 taper for every four feet, but the operators stay within .003 for six months, the tolerance will be changed to .003. If the company finds that after two years they can grind them to within .001, that will become the new tolerance. The ultimate result is that there will be no variation in the spindles at all. In other words, no taper. Such continuous improvement is beginning to occur on a regular basis. If one manufacturer can do it, others had better do it also, or soon there will be only one manufacturer in business.

The decisions about the feasibility and desirability of continuous improvement all involve human sensing. For example, more improvement may be possible, but only at a prohibitive cost. Or, more improvement may be possible, but only by reducing productivity 30 percent. Such a decision may not therefore be feasible.

Both in industry and education, human sensing is less accurate than nonhuman sensors when measuring a product. However, since process has become just as important as product in industry, the use of human sensing is accepted as a part of the quality functions. That has always been true in schools. The challenge for both is to improve the nature and use of human sensing.

Reallocation of Resources

Resources are defined as both material, monetary and otherwise, and human. When the reallocation of resources is discussed, there is as much emphasis on the human element as there is on the material element. If anything, the human element gets the most emphasis. That is because the human resources of a school are more stable than the material resources, especially the monetary resources. Funds for education are constantly going up and down according to the dictates of the state legislatures and the federal government. Therefore, in keeping with the long-term perspective of total quality management, the emphasis is on the reallocation of human resources. More money has not significantly improved education in the view of the public. The definition of quality is that it meets and exceeds the expectations of its clients. Education has not met its clients' expectations with the use of more resources. It seems logical that what is needed in educational leadership is a strategy to reallocate resources.

Reallocation is based on the belief that education, like private enterprise, cannot depend on additional resources as the basic method of improvement. Economic and political indicators and trends suggest that education is going to be asked to improve before any substantial public resources, both state and national, will be considered.

Since the hope of additional resources is chancy at best, education has a better opportunity to improve its quality by planning to reallocate current resources, as opposed to planning based on an assumption of additional resources. The current paradigm in relation to school planning looks like the following diagram.

$$\left. \begin{array}{l} \text{Additional standards} \\ \text{Additional mandates from public/government} \\ \text{Additional expectations self/societal} \end{array} \right\} = \text{Additional resources}$$

The future paradigm, based on total quality experience and definition, will look like the following diagram.

$$\left.\begin{array}{l} \text{Additional standards} \\ \text{Additional mandates from public/government} \\ \text{Additional expectations self/societal} \end{array}\right\} = \begin{array}{c} \text{Reallocation of} \\ \text{resources} \end{array}$$

A second premise of this quality indicator is that schools would have a better chance of continuous improvement if current resources were reallocated to more closely correlate with the philosophy of total quality management. This premise has nothing to do with the level of resources, but instead questions the entire philosophy and reasoning for the way educational resources are currently allocated. The aims of the reallocation of resources are:

(1) To move more resources to the operations level (the classroom level)
(2) To change the roles of both administration and teachers so that more integration occurs on an ongoing basis
(3) To shift educational process decision making downward from district and building level administration to the source of schooling (the operational level, the classroom)

The total quality approach to the reallocation of resources assumes that teachers and lower level administrators will assume a professional stance and approach to this use of resources. The approach also assumes that all levels of the organization will be intrinsically motivated to allocate resources for the benefit of the school, and will not let self-interest dominate their thinking and decision making.

Whether or not this assumption is accurate and valid is a "chicken and egg" argument. Some say that education must have "true professionals" in the classroom before administrators will be willing to empower teachers equivalent to what is considered in other professions as an appropriate decision-making role. Others, like me, argue that teaching must be professionalized first by empowerment, in order to raise the performance level of the role. In industry, workers on the line at the operational level have accepted the additional responsibility and have contributed both expertise and responsiveness to the aims of their organization. Teachers are at least as well equipped to do the same for schools.

QUALITY CHARACTERISTIC 8—QUALITY TEAMS

The Role of Teams

Educational program quality will not happen with only the administration involved. Not only must teachers be involved, but teachers and administrators must be involved together. As schools become more involved in the quality movement, they discover the benefits of having people at all levels of the school organization working together in teams.

There are two types of teams needed for educational program quality leadership—project teams and guidance teams.

Project Teams

The main agenda of the project team is to improve the work process in curriculum and instruction or the connection thereof by (1) finding solutions to problems, and (2) finding ways to improve. Their hidden agenda is that they are the instruments of widespread education. They plant the seeds of "quality leadership." They are the classroom through which the entire school operation learns lessons such as the following.

- How to blend teamwork and scientific methods—Project team members learn how to work as a team and how to improve processes using scientific tools and techniques. The team leader also learns how to plan and manage a project, how to conduct effective meetings, and how to facilitate group processes. All members can carry these skills beyond the project.
- Where guidance teams fit in—Through regular meetings with the project teams, the managers guiding the project also learn about the scientific approach to problem solving. In addition, they learn how to coach and inquire about project team progress. They begin to understand the exciting, successful side of projects as well as the tedious, confused, and unsuccessful side.
- Moving the decisions downward—In most schools, decisions are made two or three hierarchical levels above where they should be made. Projects provide an opportunity to empower groups at the teaching level—the groups that connect

curriculum with instruction — with the authority to decide on changes.

- Making improvements is not easy — Everyone in the school organization learns that the achievement of ever-improving quality is not easy. Administrators learn they need to be patient.
- How to develop internal experts — Schools need to develop a network of individuals trained to provide technical assistance to project teams and other quality improvement efforts. These specialists are referred to as "quality advisors."
- How to expand effort — Other people outside and inside the school organization learn from the project team's work through presentations, and by participating in the changes resulting from the team's effort. To aid this process, project teams are typically asked to make presentations to people outside the school, at regional and state meetings, and so forth.
- How to balance projects — Projects should be balanced so that (1) at least half the projects have the potential to realize significant student achievement improvement, measurable in some scientific method; (2) at least half, but not necessarily all, of the projects involve teachers; and (3) at least one is a collaboration between departments, or buildings.

The project selection checklist[22] summarizes the main points of this discussion. Using it can help administrators and others to select projects with a good chance of success (see Figure 7.1). Currently, schools have subject area departments and grade level meetings. These organizational schemes can continue to be used in education program quality. All schools need to do is change their function so that the pursuit of quality is the primary mission.

Team Members

Team members should remember that the administration has indicated its interest in quality by establishing the project team. Therefore, team members should consider their participation as a priority

---

[22]Scholtes, P. R. et al. 1989. *The Team Handbook, How to Use Teams to Improve Quality.* Madison, WI: Joiner Associates, Inc., pp. 3–4.

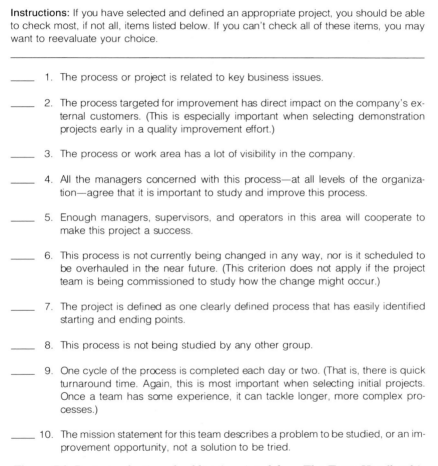

Instructions: If you have selected and defined an appropriate project, you should be able to check most, if not all, items listed below. If you can't check all of these items, you may want to reevaluate your choice.

_____ 1. The process or project is related to key business issues.

_____ 2. The process targeted for improvement has direct impact on the company's external customers. (This is especially important when selecting demonstration projects early in a quality improvement effort.)

_____ 3. The process or work area has a lot of visibility in the company.

_____ 4. All the managers concerned with this process—at all levels of the organization—agree that it is important to study and improve this process.

_____ 5. Enough managers, supervisors, and operators in this area will cooperate to make this project a success.

_____ 6. This process is not currently being changed in any way, nor is it scheduled to be overhauled in the near future. (This criterion does not apply if the project team is being commissioned to study how the change might occur.)

_____ 7. The project is defined as one clearly defined process that has easily identified starting and ending points.

_____ 8. This process is not being studied by any other group.

_____ 9. One cycle of the process is completed each day or two. (That is, there is quick turnaround time. Again, this is most important when selecting initial projects. Once a team has some experience, it can tackle longer, more complex processes.)

_____ 10. The mission statement for this team describes a problem to be studied, or an improvement opportunity, not a solution to be tried.

Figure 7.1 _Project selection checklist (reprinted from_ The Team Handbook_)._

responsibility, not an intrusion on their real jobs. Quality projects must be viewed as a part of the teacher's real job.

Members are responsible for contributing as fully to the project as possible, sharing their knowledge and expertise, and participating in all meetings and discussions, even if the topic is not in their area. They need to understand all parts of the process. This is a holistic approach that is characteristic of the entire total quality effort. Team members must also carry out their assignments between meetings, such as data gathering, observing, writing reports, and so on.

Doing the Groundwork

Before the quality project team gets down to work, the following things must be done.

Identify the Goals

What changes are expected to result from this project? These changes are not necessarily stated in numerical terms, but can be described using terms like "increase," "decrease," or "sharply decrease."

Prepare a Mission Statement

A proper mission statement enables a project team to set boundaries on the project, know what is and isn't within their jurisdiction, understand where the project fits into the organization's overall improvement effort, and have a clear idea of where they should begin.

The statement should tell the team:

- what process or problem to study
- what boundaries or limitations there are, including limits on time and money
- what magnitude of improvement they are expected to make
- when they are scheduled to begin the project and, if appropriate, the target date for completion
- what authority they have to call in coteachers or outside experts, request equipment or information normally inaccessible to them, and make changes to the process
- who is on the guidance team

- how often they are expected to meet with the guidance team and the date of the first joint meeting

Determine the Resources

What training is needed? Budget? Equipment? Which in-house or external specialists will be needed to advise the team? How much time must be allotted so that team members will be able to complete the project? How will their normal work get done? By whom?

Select the Team Leader

The project team leader is often the administrator or supervisor responsible for the building or department or grade level where most of the changes are likely to occur. This person should be someone interested in solving the problems that prompted this project, someone who is reasonably good at working with individuals and groups.

Assign the Quality Advisor

The guidance team should assign a quality advisor to work with the team leader. The quality advisor is someone experienced in working with groups, someone who knows and can teach others the basic scientific tools. The quality advisor and team leader will review the mission statement and facilitate the project's development.

Select the Project Team

The administrative team should collaborate with the team leader and quality advisor to determine what disciplines, grade levels, etc., should be represented on the team. Ideally, team members should represent each area affected by the improvements and each level of employees affected. Do not let the team get too large. Not everyone who can contribute something worthwhile to the team need be on the team. Project team members can always consult with them if desirable. Also, project team membership does not have to represent all levels of the chain of command. Mixing levels is, however, an effective way to improve communication and leadership methods.

Don't expect team members to take on the project work as additional work; adjust workloads to make time for the project.

Guidance Team

The guidance team is a group of administrators and other key leaders who oversee and support the activities of project teams. Key leaders could mean superintendents, central office personnel, principals, counselors, teachers, or any other person who fits the description of leader.

The guidance team has three to six members with diverse skills and resources (teachers or other nonadministrators who have needed qualifications will be included), who all have a stake in the chosen process. These people must possess the authority to make changes in the process under study, as well as the clout and courage to do so.

One or two of the administrators on the guidance team should be those who have established authority and responsibility regarding the process they want studied. One problem in schools is that too many decisions are made by the wrong people. Decisions should be made by principals and teachers—the people working with the daily process—rather than by superintendents and boards. The guidance team concept will only work if superintendents, middle managers, and principals are willing to let go of some responsibilities and authority. The project team is the perfect opportunity for superintendents and other administrators to learn to delegate control and pass decision making to those closest to the learning process—teachers and principals.

Guidance team members do not conduct the actual project; they guide the efforts of the project team. They appoint the project team leader, and together with that leader they determine the project's boundaries and select the other team members it needs to be successful.

The duties of the guidance team occur in two phases—preparation for the project, and execution of the project. Before beginning the project, the guidance team should:

- identify the project's goals
- prepare a mission statement
- determine needed resources
- select the team leader
- assign the quality advisor
- select the project team

During the project, the guidance team should:

- meet regularly with the project team
- develop and improve systems that allow team members to bring about change; this includes opening communication lines between the team and the rest of the department, grade level, school building, and school system
- when necessary run interference for the project team, representing its interests to the rest of the school system
- ensure that changes made by the team are followed up; implement changes the project team is not authorized to make

The responsibilities of the guidance team are not finished until the changes are introduced, the improvements accomplished, or the new methods systemized and the project officially completed. This may take anywhere from several weeks to over a year.

Choosing the Players

Educational program total quality is everybody's concern. However, there are key players in carrying out the process. These key players are:

- Project team members—the people, mostly teachers, who form the majority of the quality project team, who carry out the assignments, and who make the improvements. These people, if enthusiastic and hard working, contribute most to the educational program's total quality. But they must be given an effective team system within which to work, and that depends on the guidance team, the team leader, and the quality advisor.
- Guidance team members—support the project team's activities, secure resources, and clear a path in the organization for the decisions that the project team makes.
- Quality advisor—is a person trained in the scientific approach and in working with groups. He/she helps keep the team on track and provides training and consulting as needed.
- Team leader—runs the project team, arranging logistical details, facilitating meetings, and so forth. The team leader will usually be a lead teacher or department head. The team leader should be reasonably good at working with individuals and groups. Ultimately, it is the leader's responsibility to create and maintain channels that enable team members to do their work.

Effective leaders share their responsibilities with other team members, and trust their group to arrive at the best answer, giving team members a chance to succeed or make mistakes on their own. They understand that the lessons members learn from experience are stronger and last longer than those that come from having the leader tell them what to do.

The team leader is the contact point for communication between the team and the rest of the school organization, including the guidance team. If any member has difficulty in being released for the project assignment, the team leader may intervene with other supervisors or administrators to resolve the conflict or seek the assistance of the guidance team. When necessary, the leader meets with the guidance team members.

The team leader serves as the official keeper of the team records, including copies of correspondence, records of meetings and presentations, meeting minutes and agendas, and charts, graphs, and other data related to the project. The team leader is formally responsible for documenting the project.

Remember that the leader is a full-fledged team member. The only difference is that the team leader may want to restrain his or her participation in discussions so that other members of the team may be more active.

But the leader also retains authority as a supervisor or administrator, so he/she can immediately implement changes recommended by the team that are within the bounds of this authority. Changes beyond these bounds must be referred to the guidance team or other appropriate levels of management.

Balancing Team Leader and Quality Advisor Roles

Administrators, team leaders, team members, and the quality advisors themselves must not think of quality advisors as the leaders or as other role players in the quality project. The quality advisor must remain, as much as possible, the outside consultant to the team.

Figure 7.2 illustrates how the proportions of active leadership taken on by the team leader and quality advisor can vary during the project.[23] The quality advisor, trained in meeting skills, may run parts of

[23]Ibid., pp. 3–11.

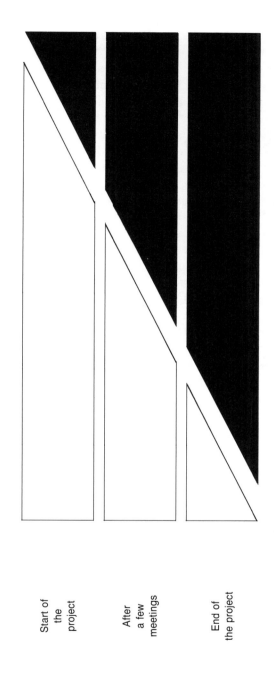

Amount of active leadership by quality advisor

Amount of active leadership by team leader (may be shared with others)

Start of
the
project

After
a few
meetings

End of
the project

Figure 7.2 *Continuum of power sharing between a team leader and a quality advisor (reprinted from* The Team Handbook).

the first team meetings, but the team leader gradually assumes more of these duties. Throughout a project, the team leader may choose to share responsibility from time to time with other team members.

The quality advisor is versed in the tools and concepts of quality improvement, including approaches that help a team have effective, productive meetings. The quality advisor is there to help facilitate the team's work—coaching team members in needed skills and tools—but not to participate directly in the team's activities.

The quality advisor's responsibilities include:

- He/she focuses on the team's process more than its product and is concerned more with how decisions are made than what decisions are made.
- He/she assists the team leader in structuring or breaking down a task into individual assignments. Most projects consist of several, or even hundreds of individual tasks performed effectively and in a planned sequence to reach the desired goal.
- He/she works with the team leader between meetings to plan for upcoming meetings. They may have to structure individual tasks, discussions, and decisions so that the team can work effectively. They revise the plans in response to suggestions from team members, the guidance teams, or day-to-day experience on the project.
- He/she studies and uses the principles of educational program quality control and helps explain these principles to the rest of the team.
- He/she helps team members to become more comfortable with statistics and to develop their own facility with the scientific approach.
- He/she teaches data collection and analysis techniques to the team, showing what conclusions may or may not be drawn from the data.
- He/she helps team members learn to graph data in ways that make the message clear, particularly to people outside the team. The quality advisor encourages the group to seek the causes of problems before identifying solutions and to distrust any decisions unsupported by valid data.
- He/she helps the group decide what data will be useful and

how best to gather data. The quality advisor works with team members and those outside the team who may be gathering and recording data to develop appropriate forms for data collection.

- He/she prepares teaching modules on various statistical approaches—with the help of a statistician if necessary—to present to the team at the appropriate time.
- He/she continually develops personal skills in facilitating, group processes, and planning. The quality advisor learns a variety of techniques to control digressive, difficult, or dominating participants, to encourage reluctant participants, and to resolve conflict among participants. The quality advisor learns when and how to employ these interventions and how to teach such skills to team members.
- He/she helps project team design, and sometimes rehearses presentations to administration.

Selecting and Training Quality Advisors

For educational program total quality to work effectively, administrators, supervisors, and teachers who serve as quality advisors must have a combination of the following:

- people skills—interpersonal communication, group process, and meeting skills; knows how to form groups, build teams, listen, resolve conflict, and give feedback
- technical skills—understands basic scientific tool, statistics, and the use of data; can organize and plan a project; understands the technical aspects of the project; can ask good questions
- training skills—can teach others all the skills described above; can give effective presentations and teach others how to do the same

School systems that have administrative personnel with these skills are ready to implement educational program total quality immediately. Those school districts that do not have such personnel must begin by selecting and training personnel in these three areas. As a last step, members of a school system should be able to check most or all of the items in Figure 7.1 before beginning.

QUALITY CHARACTERISTIC 9—
FLATTENING THE HIERARCHY

Remember, the rationale for the flattening of the hierarchy is based on self inspection at the operator level and the total quality management concept. This would mean that the teachers have equal responsibility for quality, reflected in their increased involvement in curriculum and instructional decision making. Of all the current quality efforts underway in industry, the flattening out of the hierarchy has the most promise for schools because the end result would be the true professionalization of teaching. If schools followed the lead of industry in creating more self inspection, there would be less need for administrators and supervisors, whose job it is to check on the performance of teachers in both curriculum and instruction. Therefore, teachers would become the curriculum developers and would be responsible for their own instructional quality. The essence of professionalization lies in the fact that the professional person decides what should be done and how best to do it. For teachers, that is curriculum and instruction.

Currently, the decisions and processes of curriculum and instruction are largely being carried out in the central offices by curriculum and instructional supervisors, coordinators, and other defined specialists. Therefore, following the industrial model, these people's decision-making roles would be shifted to the teachers. There would still need to be facilitator functions that would have to accompany curriculum and staff development efforts, but the number of outside specialists would decrease if and when decision-making responsibilities were transferred to the teaching staff.

This approach could only be applied to education if resources — particularly money for salaries and positions — found at the various hierarchical levels were diverted to the teacher level. The additional money would not be used to increase teacher salaries, but to create more teaching positions. With the creation of more teaching positions, regular instruction could be occurring at all times, even when some staff members were out of the classroom for curriculum or staff development.

This arrangement would solve a current educational problem that has not been successfully addressed under the current organizational structure. That problem is how to get quality time for curriculum development and staff development. With the additional staff available, teachers could be involved in both activities on an ongoing basis without the need for substitute teachers. There would always be sufficient teachers available to adequately teach the students on a reasonable teacher/pupil ratio. The current problem of inadequate instruction (babysitting) by part time substitutes would be eliminated.

Figure 7.3 shows the change in philosophy and resources.

As you can see, a school system could hire six additional teachers and still have $20,000 left over.

Is this approach feasible? It is working for industry, and their workforce is not nearly as well educated as the teaching staffs of American schools.

The flattening out of the hierarchy and the resultant professionalization of teaching would also create new approaches to the instructional leadership of the principal. Under current educational paradigms, the schools are attempting to create principal instructional leadership by giving noninstructional duties to assistants, or by delegating curriculum development to central office specialists. In this case, the assumption is that the principal does not have to be involved in curriculum development to be effective in its monitoring. That is a shaky assumption at best.

CURRENT ORGANIZATIONAL PARADIGM	NEW PARADIGM
Three curriculum coordinators Average salary—$50,000 Total salaries—$150,000	1 curr./staff dev. Salary—$50,000
Two staff dev. coordinators Average salary—$50,000 Total salaries—$100,000	Teaching staff responsible for curr. and staff dev. (thirty-six teachers best)
Total administrative salaries—$250,000	Aver. salary $30,000 Total salaries—$1,080,000
Teaching staff (thirty teachers) Average salary—$30,000 Total salaries—$900,000	
Total Costs Admin. salaries—$250,000 Teachers' salaries—$900,000	*Total Costs* Admin. salaries—$50,000 Teachers' salaries—$1,080,000
TOTAL $1,150,000	TOTAL $1,130,000

Figure 7.3 Flattening the hierarchy.

In the new nonhierarchical model, the curriculum and instructional responsibilities would be shared by the principal and the teachers. This implies more trust in the teachers. It also implies that curriculum and staff development matters would be a regular assignment of all teachers. Needless to say, it is implied that the additional six teachers shown in Figure 7.3 make that additional involvement feasible. This is certainly desirable because it brings the total responsibility for the curriculum and instructional program inside the building. It also means that the people who are there in the building every day together will provide the leadership together. That eliminates one of the current weaknesses of both curriculum and staff development efforts in schools—they are too often planned and developed by people who are not in the building enough to know the culture or needs of the students, staff, or community.

The most significant potential of this structure is that it makes the bridging of the curriculum and instructional gap feasible if not likely. Currently, curriculum is developed by administration, while instruction is provided by the teachers. Therein lies the gap. The ownership by the teachers is not always there, so their instruction does not always reflect the planned curriculum. On the other hand, outside administrators, such as curriculum specialists, are not responsible for the monitoring of instruction. Therefore, curriculum and instruction are often nonrelated. By putting the responsibility for curriculum development and instruction (curriculum implementation) into the building, the possibility of bridging the gap is made easier, and more likely.

The economic motivation has implications for schools also. Companies become "leaner and meaner" so that the stockholders can reap bigger dividends, and thus be more satisfied with the company, continue to invest in it, and insure its survival. If schools can show that they are "leaner and meaner," then the chances of passing tax levies, and thus securing their economic survival as well as the increased opportunity for quality, are better. Taxpayers may not be shareholders in the public schools, but they are stakeholders. Since stakeholders can vote, a school's attention to their satisfaction is as important as a private company's attempt to please its stockholders.

Figure 7.4 represents the traditional school organizational structure. This type of structure has the following characteristics:

(1) It is authority-based.
(2) It is based on the decision-making function.

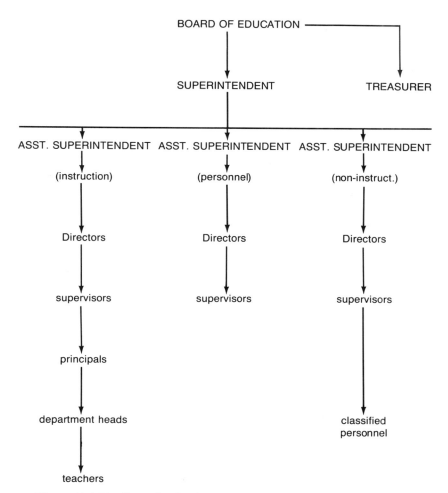

Figure 7.4 Traditional school organizational structure (eight levels).

(3) It emphasizes top down communications.

(4) It emphasizes division of labor.

(5) It is based on job descriptions.

(6) The hierarchy does not include students because students have no decision-making authority.

(7) The hierarchy does not include parents/community because neither group has decision-making authority directly. It is implied that they are represented by the board of education.

(8) It has multiple layers.
(9) It implies a closed-system definition of goals, standards, and evaluation procedures.
(10) It implies that school systems are rational organizations that have total control of the conditions that affect the organization.
(11) It emphasizes a chain of command and control in decision making and communication.

Figure 7.5 represents the organizational structure needed for total quality management. This type of organizational structure has the following characteristics:

(1) It is service driven.
(2) It is based on process and tasks.
(3) It emphasizes cross-function communication.
(4) It emphasizes teamwork and cross functions.
(5) It is based on the organizational flow charts.
(6) The clients of the school (students, parents/guardians, potential employers, higher education institutions, and the society) are prime decision makers.
(7) The organization strives for flatness (eliminates layers).
(8) Clients define and evaluate organizational quality.
(9) It implies that school systems are nonrational organizations that must share control with the external clients.
(10) It deemphasizes the chain of command and control in decision making and communication.

Flow Charts

Flow charts are the most effective way to respond to the operational definition of quality: that is, that quality is meeting and exceeding the needs and expectations of the clients.

For schools, there are multiple flow charts, each one representing the attempt to meet the needs of a specific client. The following flow charts show how the school system responds to its individual clients. Figure 7.6 shows students, Figure 7.7 shows parents/guardians, Figure 7.8 shows potential employers, Figure 7.9 shows higher education, and Figure 7.10 shows society.

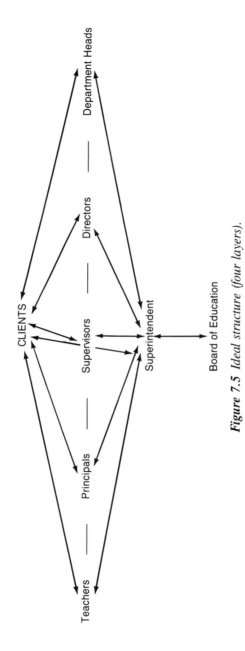

Figure 7.5 Ideal structure (four layers).

139

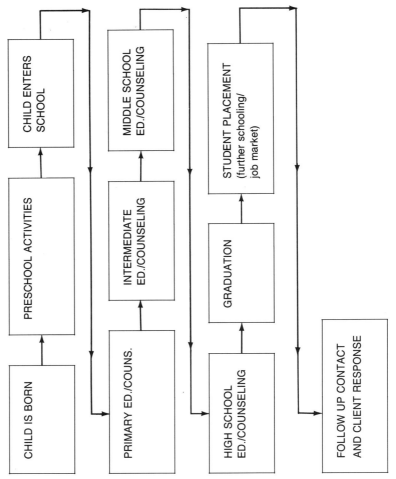

Figure 7.6 Flow chart with student as client.

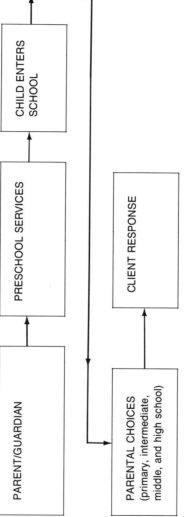

Figure 7.7 Flow chart with parent/guardian as client.

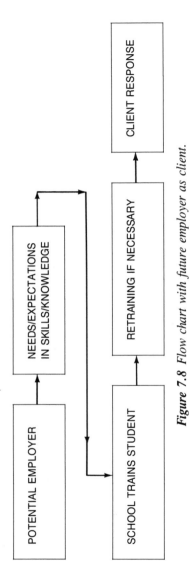

Figure 7.8 Flow chart with future employer as client.

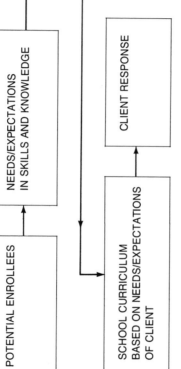

Figure 7.9 Flow chart with higher education as client.

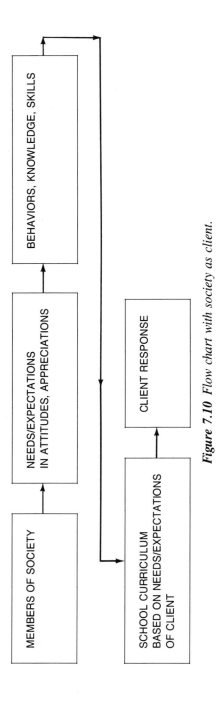

Figure 7.10 Flow chart with society as client.

144

The major reason for the emphasis on flow charts is that they are the most effective method of addressing the internal quality question which is, "How can I make your job more effective?" Job descriptions do not address this question or any of the other relevant notions connected with total quality management. Therefore, they are of little value in the pursuit of continuous improvement.

Two Views of Human Nature

Figure 7.11 represents two views of human nature. The column entitled "Prevailing System" denotes the assumptions upon which the traditional organization is based. The column called "Transformation Needed" represents the assumptions upon which total quality management is based.

Those people experienced in organizational development know that the prevailing system is deeply entrenched. The transformation will not take quickly. People are more used to competing and blaming than they are to cooperating and helping. Regression may occur during the initial phases of the transformation. For those who persevere, continuous improvement is a feasible reality.

QUALITY CHARACTERISTIC 10—NATURAL WORK GROUPS

Most school organizations are still mired in the "quality control department" way of thinking, which private industry found to be ineffective. Using the industrial parallel in schools, the production people are the teachers. Sometimes, in large school systems, where there is a large and influential central office, the principal is placed here also. The quality people are the board of education, the superintendent, and the central office administrators and supervisors, such as the curriculum, instruction, testing, and staff development specialists. All the difficulties and weaknesses that were described in the previous discussions on industries are also present in current school organizations.

So what is missing? How could schools adapt and effectively use natural work groups? Let's look at what is missing first.

Cross-Sectional Functioning

The school's product, the student, is completed only after the entire schooling process is finished. In the case of the public schools, that is

II. The Social Group (Organization)

	I	II	III	IV	V	VI
	Economics	Management Style	Result to Individual	Outcome for Organization	Predicted Results	Chances for Survival
Prevailing System	Competition	Supervision	I win. You lose.	Suboptimization	Nonexistent	Nonexistent
Transformation Needed	Cooperation	Team Synergy	I win! You win! We win!	Optimization	High Probability of Success	High

Figure 7.11 Two views of human nature.

high school graduation. Therefore, the study and solution to quality problems must involve personnel from the entire school community. Quality must be approached from a K–12 perspective, in a districtwide approach. Natural work groups must be made up of people from all the different buildings of the school district. There will no longer be distinct high school curriculum problems or primary curriculum problems, but district or school curriculum problems. They are interrelated and should be addressed as such.

Teacher Included in Quality Analysis

To follow the industrial model, schools must begin assuming that the teachers, the operators of the school industry, know at least as much about the process being studied as the designers (curriculum specialists) or the inspectors (instructional and testing specialists). If the teachers need some additional professional development in order to participate in the quality analysis, then the organization will provide it to them as part of their natural work. Of course, the teachers' involvement in the quality analysis is part of their natural work function also.

Staff Development Based on Quality Problem or Improvement

Currently, many schools base their entire staff development program on the pursuit of generic topics. Usually, these are nationally identified needs that are supposed to improve education overall. However, there is usually very little analysis of whether or not these programs are needed in particular school districts.

A better approach to continual improvement is to base the staff development, as does industry, on the particular problems or processes that have been identified as crucial to the improvement of a process or product.

Natural Work Group of the Teacher Includes the Quality Components (Curriculum, Instruction, Testing)

This means that teachers must be involved in the design and delivery of all three of these aspects of schooling. Currently, most teachers are only totally involved in the instructional phase. Involvement here means making decisions on what content makes up the curriculum, what are appropriate teacher and learner behaviors, what tests or assessments will be used, and how they will be applied to individual students. If the teachers do not have the expertise to be involved in all of these decisions, then the school must provide them with the professional development opportunities that will make their involvement successful.

Elimination of the Extracurricular Nature of Curriculum and Staff Development

If curriculum and professional development are going to be a part of the teachers' natural work group, then it must be a part of their regular day, and it must not render their teaching role ineffective because of work overload. This will require quality time for these endeavors through the use of released time, extended contracts, and the reallocation of human resources at the teacher level to make this paradigm switch feasible.

To follow the industrial example of the use of natural work groups to improve quality, schools must put more trust in teacher expertise. If the expertise is not there among the teaching staff, schools must either change staff to provide it, or develop the expertise of their staffs through professional development programs.

The poignant points of this whole discussion on natural work groups are these. Quality must become everybody's job. Quality is not a departmental function. It is an organizational function. The work groups must be a cross section of the organization, and must include teachers as an integral part of the decision-making process.

Most important of all, if the teachers don't have the expertise to participate in natural work groups, then they must be trained to the point where they can contribute. To do anything else will eliminate the opportunity to pursue continuous improvement through the use of natural work groups as defined by their use in private industry.

QUALITY CHARACTERISTIC 11—EMPOWERMENT

Teachers are not looking for more work, and they will not accept more work unless they believe it will lead to some improvement in their profession. The empowerment of teachers will require them to do more work than they currently perform. This change must professionalize teachers, rather than simply giving them more procedural tasks to perform.

Key Elements

The key elements to teacher empowerment are (1) training, (2), time, (3) money, and (4) ongoing district support. To accomplish these elements, teachers must be given access to current or state-of-the-art information on which to base decisions. This information should center on the following topics:

- consensus building
- brainstorming
- creative problem solving
- group dynamics
- leadership skills

Key steps in the process of teacher empowerment are:

(1) Leadership is critical in cultivating participatory management, and principals need training to act in that role.
(2) Empowering teachers with more decision-making authority requires that a critical mass of teachers be willing to spend extra time and energy.
(3) Staff development is another critical factor. Training in communication skills, in conflict resolution, and in team building are especially important. "When we get to the planning of our vision," one teacher said, "we find we need more skills."
(4) Trust among teachers and between teachers and administrators is a necessary first step in the empowerment of teachers. Empowerment will not happen as long as teachers are waiting for the other shoe to drop.

Empowerment to Achieve Responsiveness

Teacher, client, and administrator involvement and responsiveness in quality policy and procedures over time is the crux of empowerment.

A school system with empowerment in the educational program is one in which the clients, staff, board, teachers, and administrators acknowledge possession of the program. The staff gives the educational program its rightful recognition and maintains its support of the program during times of adversity.

The total quality research and literature clearly states that the workers must be partners in quality. In schools, the workers are the students. The people in the schools who work most closely with the students are the teachers, defined in total quality as first level management. If these two groups are not responsive to the quality program, it cannot function effectively.

From the ideal philosophical point of view, responsiveness should derive from a feeling of ownership. However, this sense of ownership is not absolutely necessary, and should not become an end in itself.

Regardless of how positive one's outlook is on education and the people who work in education, there will be times when a universal sense of ownership will not occur. If total ownership is always a prerequisite, then quality will be difficult to achieve. No organization, no matter how people oriented it is, can run such a risk.

However, in the normal workings of organizations, empowerment produces a sense of ownership, which in turn produces responsiveness. This organizational state can be encouraged through the involvement of teachers in curriculum and instructional decision making, and the maintenance of a constant flow of vital information among teachers and administrators. Opinions of teachers and middle management must be valued, and the staff must be kept informed of the school's quality effort. Staff must be involved in the establishing of the school focus, so that they can perceive a congruency of personal and organizational mission, as well as an organizational commitment to personnel that is commensurate with employee commitment to the organization. Quality time must also be provided for educational matters such as curriculum development, teacher professional development, equitable pay for educational work, and recognition of contribution to the quality effort.

Organizational Responsiveness

For total quality to occur in schools, responsiveness to empowerment must be organizationally centered. Good teachers already have responsiveness to their own classrooms. Also, principals have responsiveness to their building management functions. However, to respond to the definitions and processes involved in quality as defined by this book, teachers and building administrators must respond to the total organizational effort.

Responsiveness and thus empowerment are already occurring in many schools. Examples are site-based management and teacher career ladders. However, policy will not produce empowerment. Professional negotiations have been bogged down in an adversarial relationship based on the protection and pursuit of self-interests. Teachers' unions are too often pursuing self-interests at the expense of educational quality. Management, board and administration, is bogged down in bureaucracy, justifying itself through control. But this control has not produced quality education. Empowerment and the responsiveness that it creates is a viable alternative in the pursuit of continuous improvement.

Specific Areas of Empowerment

Curriculum

The teacher is the individual in charge of delivering on the school's curriculum and instructional expectations. This delivery is a complex, professional task, and teachers will only deliver these organizational expectations if they feel a sense of ownership and/or responsiveness for this task. People feel ownership for those aspects of the organization in which their role plays an integral part. That is why teachers feel so much ownership for the teaching process. It is the mainstream of their professional existence. It is what they do for six or more hours a day.

If school systems expect that teachers are going to develop the same sense of ownership and responsiveness to curriculum, then the process of curriculum design and development must take on more of the characteristics of teaching. It must become part of the natural work function of teachers. For example, it must be done during quality time. In addition, every teacher affected by curriculum content must be given the opportunity for input during the development process. As significant as the total input is the requirement that this input be based on consistent information and communication. In other words, whether a teacher was a workshop participant or only involved during the staff input phase, discussion and decisions were based on the same information.

Principal Leadership

If a school is going to create and maintain teacher empowerment, the principal must adopt a servitor leadership style. This style is characterized by the leader serving the needs of the client system. It is the only leadership style consistent with empowerment. If the principal continues to use leadership styles that emphasize advocacy or troubleshooting, the implication is that control has not been relinquished. That position is inconsistent with empowerment. The very definition of empowerment insinuates that the teachers will be assuming more professional responsibilities, therefore assuming more leadership. The principal will be performing the tasks necessary to allow this teacher leadership to take place.

The two assumptions that must be present for servitor leadership style to work are:

(1) The teaching staff has the experience and knowledge level necessary to make decisions and solve problems.

(2) The teaching staff is at least as knowledgeable as the principal on the question.

If these two conditions are not present, but the principal wishes to use servitor leadership style, then the training to bring the staff to the necessary level should be initiated and completed.

According to Sergiovanni,[24] less administrative leadership and teacher professionalism go hand in hand. Servitor behavior could be defined as less administrative leadership within the context of power and control over teachers.

For empowerment to work, teachers must know that leadership is in their realm of responsibility, and that this newly empowered responsibility is permanent. That means that it is theirs as a part of their professional status, and is not something that is theirs temporarily because the principal has decided to give it to them. If power is in the hands of teachers only because the principal has decided to give it to them, then it logically follows that the principal can take it away as quickly as he granted it. Therefore, the implication is that teachers had better use their power in such a way that it pleases the administration. If not, it

---

[24]Sergiovanni, T. J. 1992. "Why We Should Seek Substitutes for Leadership," *Educational Leadership*, 49(Feb.):41.

might be taken away. This is not empowerment, it is an attempt at forming a rubber-stamp committee. True empowerment can only be meaningful if it is the result of the organizational professionalization of teaching.

The principal servitor leadership style takes a lot of courage when considered under the operational definition presented within this text. The result of servitor leadership is that the principal will be blamed for actions of his/her teachers that were not effective or which caused some other problem. Being a servitor requires confidence that, in the long run, empowerment will produce better decision making and organizational management. The principal who has this belief will not abandon empowerment at the first sign of trouble. After all, there is a lot of trouble now with the so-called "strong" leadership styles.

Empowerment through Transformation

In the educational literature, empowerment means primarily the following.

(1) Teachers will have increased roles in decision making at the building level. Therefore, there will be an effort to foster teacher development.
(2) Teachers will be engaged in more problem solving together.
(3) There will be more collaboration among teachers and between teachers and administrators.
(4) The culture will be more professional in nature.

From the quality perspective, empowerment means that there will be more self responsibility for the quality of work. Therefore, in this book, empowerment is classified under the reallocation of resources because teacher and principal empowerment cannot occur under the current administrative structure of schools.

The current notion of pursuing empowerment within schools centers around transitional leadership principles. In transitional environments, the belief is that a transition of power from administration to teachers is occurring. The implications are that the administration is taking the lead in effecting this transition, and therein lies the fallacy of this notion of empowerment. The administration is still in control of the process, therefore the success of this type of empowerment depends on administrative leadership. The administrative leadership can create the transitional empowerment. Therefore, it can take it away.

The kind of change needed to unleash the potential of empowerment could better be described as transformational. This transformation must affect not only the role of teachers, but also the role of administrators. When the transformation is complete, it should be something that the administration could not rescind.

Said another way, empowerment must not be dependent upon leadership for it to occur. Instead of emphasizing leadership to achieve empowerment, professionalism should be the emphasis.

Transition in empowerment depends on administrative leadership. Transformation in empowerment depends on teacher professionalism.

Teachers currently lack the time to devote to organizational planning and operations, as well as a certain expertise that will be necessary for empowerment. This necessary expertise includes knowledge of curriculum design and development, student testing and assessment analysis, collaboration motivation and skills, and organizational decision making and problem solving.

Neither the resource need of time nor the development of the expertise needed can be accomplished with the current educational structure. Empowerment can only be achieved by reallocating resources to allow teachers more time to pursue the new organizational mission of empowerment. This means a reduction in the number of administrators and an increase in the number of teachers so that the role/function of the teacher includes organizational responsibilities as well as classroom teaching.

Also, there must be intensive teacher development in the areas of curriculum design and development, test/assessment data analysis, and group process skill development and team development that is ongoing to accommodate turnover of personnel.

The current state of affairs in the pursuit of empowerment for teachers is a hybrid. It plays with transitional activities that do not attack the basic obstacle to teacher empowerment; that is, the reallocation of resources. Either empowerment must happen through the transformation of decision making and problem solving, or schools should abandon the notion of teacher empowerment and work toward a distinct division of labor where teachers would only be asked to teach and would not be involved in the other operations of the school such as planning and curriculum development. That is a new paradigm, not to my liking, but preferable to the current paradigm which pretends to accept teachers as professionals but does not allocate resources accordingly.

If the quality perspective is to be followed, resources must be reallocated so that the transformation to responsibility for one's own work is feasible. The reallocation must accept that time is the most vital resource in the school structure. Teachers' time must be reallocated. Also, resources relating to teacher development must concentrate on the skills that teachers will need to responsibly use their new-found organizational empowerment.

QUALITY CHARACTERISTIC 12—ABANDONMENT

For schools, the "frontier philosophy" has historically prevailed as the means of improvement in both curriculum and instruction. The growth in curriculum offerings and in the number of people administering and teaching in schools has been large and continual. Abandonment, as it is being used in industry, has applications to both school curriculum and personnel.

In curriculum, the content offerings have grown to the point where focus and constancy of purpose have become vague. Something must be abandoned to recapture focus in curriculum content. Constancy of purpose is not present because of the constant additions and alterations in curricular offerings due to fadism, government and societal mandates, and environment needs.

Three abandonment options are possible to reassert focus and constancy of purpose. First, schools could abandon the current instructional structure: that is, nine months of schooling a year, for thirteen years. If this structure was abandoned in favor of one with more instructional time, then content would not have to be abandoned. A second option is to abandon curriculum content. This could be done by reestablishing focus as the determinant of what is abandoned and what is kept. A third option is to abandon the focus on student recall of content and substitute a focus on research skills.

In personnel, the reduction in the emphasis on outside inspection and the resultant lessening of the need for middle management that has occurred in industry could be applied to schools. This would mean a reduction in supervisors whose function is to monitor (inspect) classroom performance of teachers and curriculum coordinators or developers. It would also mean a reduction in other administrative positions that do not contribute directly to the instructional (operational) program of the schools.

Needless to say, the salary and medical cost savings that have occurred in industry would also occur in education. Such savings could be applied to the productivity aspects of the school operation, the instructional program.

Develop a System of Abandonment

A big obstacle to effective educational program quality is the fact that schools are being asked to do many tasks that are not central to basic education. Some of these added curricula I support. Some I oppose. The significant point is that the public schools are being asked to solve societal problems in addition to doing a better job in the traditional educational areas. In an attempt to respond to all the demands and pressures, schools are adding both curriculum and instructional programs. Seldom are schools abandoning anything. But the time and expertise of school personnel is already overtaxed. Not only is the continual addition of programs no longer feasible, but a concerted effort to abandon some tasks is desirable. Two approaches to the process of abandonment are feasible. First of all, abandon those programs and tasks not needed for effective education, and abandon other programs that are a low priority based on their contribution to the focus of the school. Secondly, only add to the school program if something of equal time and resources can be abandoned. To illustrate the current plight of schools, consider the following.

Public schools in America today are expected to:

- teach good nutrition habits
- train students in pulmonary-coronary resuscitation
- give specialized instruction for the hard of hearing, the blind, and the neurologically impaired
- treat the emotionally disturbed
- train the mentally retarded
- teach the gifted
- do eye testing
- give inoculations
- teach first aid procedures
- provide pregnancy counseling

- assist in disease prevention
- inculcate morals, ethics, and values
- stress drug, alcohol, and tobacco abuse
- help students develop political know-how
- develop civic responsibility
- provide sex education
- maintain birth information and age certification data
- provide instruction in good health care
- teach driver training
- provide civil rights and racial tolerance
- foster integration
- teach the principles of free enterprise
- assist in career planning
- provide career information
- detect and report child abuse
- teach telephone manners and etiquette
- eradicate head lice, scabies, and other diseases
- assist in charity fund-raising
- provide vocational training
- build economic awareness
- serve hot lunches and breakfasts
- dispense surplus milk
- do job placement
- stress bicycle safety and pedestrian safety
- promote physical fitness
- assist bilingual language development
- counsel delinquents
- foster metric education
- provide transportation
- teach consumer education
- counsel students with problems
- follow due process procedures
- protect student privacy
- teach humaneness and individual responsibility
- eliminate sex discrimination
- develop an appreciation of other people and other cultures
- promote the uses of information
- develop the ability to reason
- build patriotism and loyalty to the ideals of democracy

- promote an understanding of the heritage of our country
- build respect for the worth and dignity of the individual
- develop skills for an entry into a specific field
- teach management of money, property, and resources
- develop curiosity and thirst for learning
- develop skills in the use of leisure time
- teach pride in work
- build a feeling of self-worth, or self-respect
- avoid religion

Schools are expected to do all of this, in addition to teaching "reading, writing, and arithmetic."

This litany grows continually with each new sociological problem that this nation or the world encounters or imagines. It shows no sign of slowing up. The problem for schools in relation to educational quality is obvious. In order for educational leaders to become the curriculum and instructional leaders that quality demands, some things that are currently receiving priority in the schools are going to have to be abandoned.

At first thought this seems like a simple enough process. But for organizations it is not. As Drucker has so well stated, "Organizations have no systematic method of abandoning anything." But schools must! Superintendents, principals, other administrators, and teachers must ask themselves and their public, "What can be abandoned so that we have time for systemwide and building-wide curriculum and instructional emphasis?" What can we abandon so that we can be curriculum and instructional leaders?

The litany of what could be abandoned may not be as long as the litany of public school tasks that was previously presented. However, the possibilities are there. Some of the major ones for consideration include, for administrators, the following.

- Monitor curriculum and instruction only if it results in adjustments.
- If monitoring does not trigger a response, don't do it.
- Utilize time-saving technology.
- Delegate decision making.
- Abandon the notion of tradition for the sake of tradition.
- Establish priorities in relation to time and monetary resources.
- Maintain the school's vision, i.e., devote energy and time only to the pursuit of the organizational vision and missions.

- Abandon tasks, processes, decisions, and products that do not contribute to the vision and missions of the school.

For teachers, some possible avenues for abandonment include the following.

- Abandon clerical tasks that have no connection with teaching or curriculum. However, care must be taken that the teacher abandonment program does not include curriculum development, diagnostic, or assessment functions. These are vital to educational quality.
- In curriculum content, examine what pupil performance objectives can be abandoned so that the course of study equals or corresponds to the amount of time allocated for its completion.

In general, four types of abandonment must occur for educational total quality management to be effective. They are characterized by the following four questions:

(1) What can administrators and supervisors abandon so that they can become better curriculum and instructional leaders?

(2) What can teachers abandon so they can spend more time on curriculum and instruction?

(3) What curriculum can be abandoned so that the vision and missions of the school receive priority?

(4) What can the organization abandon so that more time and energy can be devoted to the vision and missions?

This question of what can be abandoned must be asked about each position in the school. In other words, what can the superintendent abandon? What can the principal abandon? What can the teachers abandon? There are two possible levels of abandonment. First, can the process be abandoned totally? If not, can the person in question abandon it personally, while keeping it as a process or task or decision by someone else in the organization?

When an organization is dealing with this question, it is wise to consider these two levels separately. First, decide what can be totally abandoned, and do it. The cycle will be complete. This will be the easiest part of the abandonment program.

In order to be a candidate for total abandonment, at least one of the following criteria must be true.

(1) This task, process, decision, or product is not necessary for the accomplishment or pursuit of the vision or the organizational missions.

(2) This task, process, decision, or product has too low a priority to receive time and attention.

Abandoning processes on a personal level while retaining them in the organization involves the delegation of authority and responsibility. However, do not assume that the reassignment of tasks will always occur downward in the organization. There are times when the vision and the missions of the organization might be better served if the reassignment of the tasks is upward in the hierarchy. The significant point of this discussion is that the responsibility be assigned to the person who can best perform this function without damaging his/her efforts toward the missions of the organization. When we are talking about abandoning things that are not contributing to the vision, we are usually talking about things auxiliary to the mission that still must be done. Almost everyone in the organization is probably overqualified to do the tasks. Therefore, it is more a matter of who can do it with the least amount of disarray, rather than who should perform this important task.

Also, this process is often a balancing of duties in relation to time. If some people in the organization are too busy, then the abandonment process occurs simply to relieve these people's work schedules.

Steps to Organizational Abandonment

(1) Clarify organizational missions.

(2) Examine organizational activities to check their contribution to the organizational missions.

(3) Abandon those activities that are not contributing to the organizational missions.

(4) Prioritize the remaining activities that are contributing to the organizational missions.

(5) Determine the resource level potential of the organization. This means asking how many of the activities prioritized above the organization can actually perform.

(6) Abandon where time and or resources demand, and where no delegation of the task is feasible.

A system of abandonment will have positive side effects. The prioritization process will verify the worthiness of a lot of what is already occurring in the organization. This in itself is worthwhile. It helps to clarify the vision and the missions, and calls attention to them. Secondly, it will tend to lay issues to rest. That is, even if some people do not like the fact that we are doing certain things, it will be seen that we have to keep doing them anyway.

Adding Programs within the Context of Abandonment

There are times when schools must add new programs. Some of these times include periods when new standards or mandates from the state or national legislatures or educational departments are introduced, or when an overwhelming evidence of a new need becomes apparent. In these instances, the abandonment process becomes one of deciding what to abandon in order to add the new program. To do this, use the prioritization process previously discussed. Remember, the formula is this—time and resources added must at least equal the time and resources abandoned.

For educational total quality management to be effective, educational leaders must spend time, energy, and resources in the curriculum and instructional realm. In order to do this, school leaders are going to have to reprioritize their function. Included in this process should be a consideration for implementing a system of abandonment. If time and diversity of tasks for school leaders is, in fact, already overwhelming, then rethinking priorities still may not allow the leader the time, resources, and energy to work effectively toward educational quality. Abandonment then becomes the only solution.

QUALITY CHARACTERISTIC 13— REDUCTION IN INSPECTION

Teacher Inspection

Have you ever thought about how antiquated the educational system of inspection and monitoring is, if taken in the context of where industry has been and is going? By industrial standards and historical development on this topic, education is somewhere in the nineteenth century. What makes this so incredible is that the educational operations in question are being performed by college graduates. Teaching is considered by many to be a professional function, whereas industrial operations have been and continue to sometimes be performed by people with little formal education. Despite this, education relies more on inspection and monitoring for quality than does industry. Putting it plainly, industry has more faith in its workers than education has in its teachers or students.

To reduce inspection and monitoring, schools need to put responsibility for quality on the shoulders of their teachers. This would mean the end of monitoring for the sake of monitoring. Principals or other administrators would only monitor if such activities produced a significant response. In other words, as in industry, monitoring would only occur when trouble arises. Think of the endless number of hours principals spend in classroom observations and follow-up conferences, only to say "keep up the good work."

Listed below are the things that would happen if education adopted less inspection and put quality responsibility on the teachers:

(1) An administrator would become more of a resource person and less of an inspector.

(2) Student testing results would be analyzed by classroom, and then given to the teachers for interpretation and action.

(3) Administrators would assist teachers through statistics, data, and other information about the students.

(4) Teachers would have to be knowledgeable about the use of assessment data, including its limitations.

(5) Poor teachers could not function in this environment of increased responsibility and expertise expectations.

(6) Administrators would have to know how to work from an expertise base of resource provider. Those who rely on authority only would have to develop expertise in facilitation to survive.

(7) The administrative hierarchy will change. Because of the reduction in inspection and monitoring, there will be fewer administrators. Instructional and curriculum decision makers will be replaced by analysts, statisticians, staff developers, model teachers, curriculum writers, facilitators, data gatherers, information synthesizers, and presenters. Superintendents and principals, and their assistants, will be the only line administrators. Anyone with the title of assistant or associate superintendent or principal would be a line decision maker for his/her superior, and would not perform staff functions.

(8) All administrators, other than superintendents and principals and their assistants, will be staff members whose purpose is to support the teachers. Their place in the hierarchy will be equal to that of the teacher.

Central to the theme of less inspection and monitoring is the belief that teachers are capable of quality responsibility. Industry has decided that workers can be responsible for quality. Education must do the same to follow the model. The question of teachers' salaries always comes up during this argument. It is a "chicken or egg" argument that usually ends with an either-or answer. The question is, do salaries have to be raised so that more competent people enter teaching, thus making it more professional? Or should the job be made more professional to begin with, thus attracting more competent people in the future? Quality education cannot wait for some future state of the teaching profession. Current teachers who are competent will accept the responsibility for quality because of the intrinsic rewards of professionalism, involvement, and autonomy. Incompetent teachers will either leave the profession or be exposed. As the profession improves, salaries will increase, better people will enter the profession, and its level of competence will make self responsibility for quality more effective.

Because of the certification requirements for teaching in all the states, education has a better chance of making this process work than industry does. There is no excuse and no reason why this change in thinking with regard to inspection and monitoring cannot be done quickly. It would save money, and more importantly, it would go a long way toward professionalizing teaching. All the profession needs is the right to make decisions in the teaching process. Industry has figured out that without responsibility at the operator level, there cannot be total quality. Education can have better quality if it places the responsibility for monitoring and inspection at the operating (teaching) level.

Student Inspection

Currently, student inspection in the schools is designed to achieve what industry calls the "old way": that is, finding the "bad ones" through grading and proficiency tests. The "bad ones" are the students who do not meet the specifications—they are outside the tolerance of the specifications, therefore they do not pass inspection.

It is interesting to note that industry is attempting to lessen its reliance on inspection to achieve quality. This is true even though industries have it within their means to control the quality of the raw material from which their product is made. For example, the publishing industry establishes standards for the paper and ink that enters its printing presses. Education has no such control over its raw material.

Students, education's raw material, enter school with diverse backgrounds and skills. This diversity is as broad as the human race itself. The notion of product inspection, as defined in industry, is not transferrable to education in any meaningful or useful form. Human beings vary so much that it is not possible to have one set of specifications for all of them. Therefore, inspection designed to meet one set of specifications is not feasible. Also, education cannot throw the bad students out. A scrap pile of unusable napkins is one thing, but a scrap pile of young people is quite another.

However, industry's efforts in changing process inspection does have implications for education. Industry's notion of building quality into the process itself could work in schools.

Current school reform efforts are based on traditional inspection thinking. For example, proficiency testing is designed to find the "bad" students. Just like in industry, this process is too late and too expensive. Neither is it client-based. Instead, it is based on specifications, complete with tolerances, that suggest that minimal levels are acceptable as a definition for quality. There are no measures built in for continuous improvement. So long as the products (students) stay within the tolerances (whatever is passing, probably 70 percent) they are defined as quality. Such standards are determined internally, without a client satisfaction definition.

If education followed current industrial leadership in inspection, it would reduce money and human resources devoted to inspection (i.e., supervision and testing) and would put more resources into improving the learning process. Ways to do this would be:

- since variation among student ability is so great, use individual learning plans for each student instead of product specifications (proficiency testing)
- more emphasis on teacher training to improve the learning process
- more money for learning materials instead of testing materials

- continuous improvement as the evaluation measure for schools, teachers, and students, as opposed to testing results based on stationary norms

SUMMARY

In this chapter we have examined six quality characteristics, all of which were geared toward reallocating human and financial resources within the school organization. The result of this reallocation will be a new school structure—one where the hierarchy is flatter, where the teaching staff is more professional, and where the whole organization has been streamlined to eliminate unnecessary practices. Thus reorganized, the school will be able to concentrate itself on implementing and maintaining a long-term process of constant improvement.

Total Quality Management Philosophy

School administrators are generally a tough bunch who have accomplished much. Their efforts have served this nation's educational systems for a long time. Most of the nation's schools have used some type of management by results approach. This is the system that nearly every major American university that trains school administrators uses as its pedagogy, and it is credited by many for the success that American education has enjoyed.

This system has, for example, Americanized the nation and gone a long way toward achieving the aims of compulsory education—a literate population to support democracy.

However, the competition involved was largely internal, based on geographical monopolies. As these geographical monopolies disappear, school systems will need to meet external competition not only from the private and parochial sector, but from other public schools.

Management by results has its own logic and consistency. It emphasizes a chain of command, originating at the top of the hierarchy and moving downward in the organizational structure. It contains a hierarchy of goals, objectives, controls, and accountability. However, it is not producing the kinds of results needed for educational program quality.

Its shortcomings are rooted in numerical goals that pay too little attention to process and systems. Its implementation has led to the following problems:

(1) Short-term thinking—Objectives reward efforts that are measurable in the short term. The near horizon gets attention even though a school's survival may depend on immeasurable activities undertaken to reach long-range goals. Top management imposes goals on middle management, middle management imposes goals

on lower management, lower management imposes goals on the teachers. This system wreaks havoc with quality and morale. Continuity from curriculum to instruction is also lost. Teachers meet goals even though they know more valuable pursuits could be utilized in the classroom.

(2) Misguided focus—If administrators and teachers truly understand the school's capability, what benefit are numerical goals? A numerical goal cannot expand the capability of the school. Only improving a system can do that. If administrators and teachers do not understand the school's capabilities, numerical goals are nothing more than guesswork that will either over or underestimate. Either way, it does little to help teachers, the school, or the parents.

(3) Internal conflicts—As each group struggles to meet objectives independently, turf wars abound. Conflicts between grade levels and departments lead to finger pointing, blame games, and excuses.

(4) Fudging the figures—Imposed, measurable goals are sometimes unattainable; they lie beyond the school system's real capability. Therefore, the employees work around the system instead of improving it. They "play the game." This charade fosters guarded communication and false figures.

(5) Greater fear—The worst shortcoming of management by results is that it creates a culture in which fear becomes the prime motivator. This state of affairs can only sustain itself for a short time before productivity is curtailed and eventually stops. People working in a state of fear do not concern themselves with continual improvement—only with continual survival.

(6) Blindness to community concerns—Management by results encourages a school to look inward rather than outward to the community and the clients of the school. Accomplishment comes from meeting numerical goals that may or may not have any priority in the community. A school system may be meeting all of its numerical goals and still not be meeting any of the expectations of the community or its client system.

Clearly, management by results is no longer sufficient to deal with the problems American schools are facing. In order to promote total quality, there is going to have to be a change in management philosophy. The exact changes that will have to occur can be found by examining quality characteristics 14, 15, 16, and 17, with special attention to the fourteen points promoted by W. Edwards Deming. These quality characteristics, which are bringing such transformation to management philosophy in industry, will be applied to education in this chapter.

QUALITY CHARACTERISTIC 14—CHANGE IN MANAGEMENT PHILOSOPHY

The new management philosophy focuses on achieving quality, which is defined as meeting and exceeding the needs and expectations of the clients. A second focus is on the acceptance and pursuit of continuous improvement as the only useful standard or goal.

The philosophy holds that example and experience teach little about theory, and that experience is not always useful knowledge. However, the new philosophy is based on the acquisition and application of knowledge. This knowledge, referred to as profound knowledge, is based on four components. In order to provide leadership for total quality, people in leadership must be able to understand and apply these four concepts.

(1) Systematic thinking—This is the interdependence of functions with their subprocesses and of the organization with its people.

(2) Theory of variation—This is the understanding of the difference between common and special causes. An understanding of variation will enable educational leaders to work toward quality within the framework of individual differences. The existence of variation is why a state of zero defects does not occur and why numerical goals are not feasible.

(3) Theory of knowledge—Only through a theory of knowledge can one understand the past and predict the future. A major component of total quality management is prediction. Only through prediction and long-term perspective can schools expect to succeed over a long period of time.

(4) Knowledge of psychology—The new philosophy is based on the understanding of people and their differences, and a commitment to applying systematic thinking to the people system. School lead-

ership's aim is to free up the potential of the different attributes of the people of the organization.

If schools continue "business as usual," without the new total quality management philosophy, we will see the following:

- a focus on each day's crises and quotas
- conformance rather than improvement
- teachers and principals blamed for most problems, with little or no understanding of systems
- teachers and principals asked to explain normal variation (common cause)
- "program of the month or year" with no constancy of purpose
- frustrated teachers and principals, powerless to change systems and unable to achieve their potential
- adversarial relationships among teachers, with their superiors, with organizations with whom they relate, and with their clients (parents, communities, etc.)
- cost of education bloated by waste
- unpredictable product and process quality
- dissatisfied consumers and clients
- underdeveloped and lost markets (not serving markets in need such as preschool and adult continual education, and losing students to private schools and home schools)
- stagnation and eroding public support, especially financial

Central to this new management will be the fourteen points of W. Edwards Deming, derived from industry and geared toward a program of total quality management:

(1) Constancy of purpose
(2) Adopt a new philosophy
(3) Cease mass inspection
(4) End price tag business
(5) Improve constantly (production and service)
(6) Institute training/retraining
(7) Institute leadership
(8) Drive out fear
(9) Break down departmental barriers
(10) Eliminate slogans, targets, and exhortations

(11) Eliminate numerical quotas

(12) Remove barriers to worker pride

(13) Institute education/self-improvement

(14) Put everyone to work to accomplish the transformation

In the discussion that follows, we will examine how each of these points applies to education.

Deming Point 1—Constancy of Purpose

The difficulties that schools would have in implementing constancy of purpose as defined by Deming[25] are twofold. First, there are difficulties in defining and sticking to a purpose, and secondly, there are difficulties in maintaining the organizational stability necessary to achieve constancy of purpose. However, both of these obstacles can be overcome. Of all of Deming's points, this one has the most utility for schools.

At first glance it would appear that the school's purpose is clear—educate students. Certainly that is clear, as a generalization. But in the complex modern world, that definition is too simplistic to be of value. For a school to know that it is producing the right product and services, it must answer the question, "What is an educated person for the present and the future?" Will the emphasis be on convergent or divergent thinking? knowledge or process? technology or basic computation? academic skills or social skills? standards or work? Are you going to sort students? So you see, the first part of constancy of purpose for schools will be to determine their purpose.

To answer this question, schools will have to spend time on the future. This means long-range thinking and planning. It means working with visioning and mission development. It means having faith in the future to the point of daring to project into the future and making commitments to that projection. Schools have experience with all of these concepts. The problem is that they have not been accompanied by long-term commitment. This is evidenced by the constant vulnerability of schools to educational fads and trends, which come and go and leave little evidence of their existence behind them. That is because innova-

---

[25]Deming, W. E. 1990. *Out of the Crisis*. Cambridge MA: Massachusetts Institute of Technology, Center for Advanced Engineering Study, p. 24.

tion, which should be a complimentary word or description, has come to mean change for the sake of change.

If you consider innovation using Deming's definition, innovation would be thought of as a constant commitment to the quality of the products and services that make up the purpose of the school. Although the innovations, when taken in isolation, may vary in content or makeup, their purpose would be constant; that is, commitment to continual improvement in the purpose of the school.

Another aspect of Deming's definition of innovation that holds out improvement potential for schools is the emphasis on training for both teachers and supervisors as a prerequisite for implementation.

It is refreshing to look upon the concept of innovation as a constant, rather than as a change process. It seems to me that education has always viewed innovation as a change process, designed to improve some aspect of schooling. But it has never been viewed as a constant process, designed to maintain constancy of purpose or continual improvement. If it was, it would not arouse the suspicion that it currently does. If all innovations were connected to the constancy of purpose of the school, which is a stable one, they would, in essence, become a regular part of the organizational effort, and would not consist of the threatening, peripheral activity that it currently does in many school organizations.

Deming's emphasis on research could easily be used by schools. The decision that needs to be made is, "Who will do the research?" If it is the school itself, then the organizational structure would need to reflect the importance of this function. If the school is going to use outside resources to conduct or adapt research, the budget should reflect this decision.

Basically, to achieve constancy of purpose, school organizations will only need to spend more time thinking about the future. The obstacles to this are the tendencies of superintendents to change jobs every three to five years. Couple this with the fact that board members constantly turn over, and the problem becomes evident.

Here is what must happen to overcome this problem. First, ethically, superintendents and board members must be willing to think beyond their tenures. There should be other safeguards beyond ethics to insure the continuity necessary for constancy of purpose.

First, policy developments and statements should include the planning and decision making that have occurred relative to constancy of purpose. Policy has continuity from superintendent to superintendent and board to board.

Second, boards and superintendents, the least stable elements of the educational community, should involve the most stable members of the educational community in the development and implementation of long-term planning. These stable members are parents, business and community leaders, and faculty. By doing this, a school district could have the stability necessary to maintain a constancy of purpose.

In summary, all a school district would need to implement Deming's constancy of purpose are (1) faith in the future, (2) policy development and implementation on the purposes of the school, and (3) the involvement of the stable members of the educational community to insure continuity.

One caution is needed. Policy has to be *living* policy. That means it must drive behavior and decision making, and must not consist simply of words in a manual gathering dust on a shelf. *Constancy of purpose cannot be fully realized unless the school is allowed to be client-driven.*

Deming Point 2—Adopt a New Philosophy

We are in a new education age. American school administration must awaken to the challenge, learn their responsibilities, and take on leadership for change. Quality must become the new religion in education. We can no longer afford poor workmanship in students, using bad learning materials, fearful and uninformed teachers, poor inservice training, and administrative job hopping. If we are to rid the schools of these practices, it will require a transformation of management philosophy.

It is hard to change after a lifelong career of doing things the same way. But in this new era of educational competitiveness, when you must compete to hold your students, school management must change in order to stay in existence. In this sense, schools are no different from the many American institutions and companies who are learning new management styles to survive in today's marketplace. World competition for both products and services has never been so intense.

Public education has been thrown into this arena through the concepts of open enrollment, parental choice, and partnerships with the private sector. The public school monopoly is being challenged everywhere, and has been removed in some areas already. President Bush has proclaimed parental choice as the cornerstone of his educational policy. The implications of this are clear—the school that survives and prospers in this era of parental choice will be the one that can produce and maintain a quality educational program.

In the face of international competition, many American companies are learning new ways to run their companies. Workers are learning how to contribute their knowledge to improving the processes to which they contribute. Chief executive officers are beginning to nurture and grow healthy corporations for long-term strength, not just short-term profit.

Schools must also begin to look toward long-term improvement. They must begin listening more to constituents who, in the end, will determine the meaning of quality for their school district. Schools will need to strive for the one thing that will, over the long term, please their constituents, and therefore make them competitive—that is, a quality educational program based on monitoring, controlling, and improvement.

Deming Point 3—Cease Mass Inspection

Cease dependence on supervision to achieve quality education. Eliminate the need for supervision on a mass basis by building quality into the teaching process in the first place.

The aim of finding the bad teachers and administrators and throwing them out is too late, too ineffective, and too costly to students and the institution through remediation efforts required to undo the damage. Quality comes not from supervision but from the improvement of the process. The old way of supervising bad quality out must be replaced by the new way of building good quality in.

Deming Point 4—End Price Tag Business

End the practice of awarding business on the basis of price tag alone. Instead, minimize total cost. Induce publishers and vendors to be actively involved with educational institutions through long-term commitments. Remember, price has no meaning without a measure of the quality being purchased.

Deming Point 5—Improve Constantly (Production and Service)

Improve constantly and forever the educational process and service to students, in order to improve quality and productivity and thus constantly decrease the cost of remediation and repetition for students.

Improvement is not a one-time effort. Everyone and every department must subscribe to the ethic of constant improvement, and management must lead the way. Only management can initiate improvement in quality and productivity. Putting out fires is not improvement of quality. Instead, schools should be asking themselves and their clients; Are we doing better than a year ago, two years ago? Is there more public support? Are students more satisfied? Has the pride and performance of the schools improved?

The pursuit of continuous improvement mandates that innovation become a stable part of the system, and more importantly, that innovation become a part of strategic planning. Planning involves continually thinking of the future. It will not be good enough to have quality based on current criteria. The stable school will be one that is searching, through innovation, for the needs and expectations that future clients will have. Those clients may be existing clients who are not aware of those future needs at the present time, or they may be people or purposes that are not currently being served by the schools, but will in the future have needs and expectations that can be fulfilled by the schools.

The car carburetor industry is no longer in existence in this country. Its demise was not due to poor quality products or services, it was due to neglect of the future. When fuel injection appeared, the market for carburetors disappeared—not because the carburetors being produced were of poor quality or were overpriced, but because a new and better process replaced it.

Schools must continually innovate so that the best educational processes will be discovered. This is the only way to maintain a stable system.

Deming Point 6—Institute Training/Retraining

Education refers to this process as inservice training, or professional development. As discussed in earlier chapters, the problem that educators have with this process is its extracurricular nature. The process is conducted after school or on weekends. This is not quality time, and it seriously reduces the effectiveness of inservice and professional development.

To understand this point of discussion, let's examine what are considered resources for teaching and learning. A list of resources would be made up largely of the following—materials, equipment, books, libraries, field trips, and teacher expertise.

Time needed to plan and accomplish the purchase of materials, equipment, and books, and to engage in field trips, is a part of the normal schedule and the budgetary process. Use of these resources will collectively make up almost the entire teaching and learning time.

But what about teacher expertise? This resource, arguably the most significant of all teaching and learning resources, is given little or no time to develop. Schools have never considered time as a vital resource. To refuse to accept time as a resource means that training and retraining of teachers and administrators will continue to occur only at the motivation and awareness level. There will not be sufficient time for in-depth training/retraining to occur.

Time for training/retraining can be achieved by concentrating resources (money and people) at the operations (teaching) level. Time as a resource is defined as scheduled, flexible, or variable periods of time available to people.

Currently in schools, the idea of time as a resource is found in administration and counseling, but not in teaching. This means that administrators and counselors can concentrate on a problem on short notice, shift their role/function emphasis quickly, and move resources around to meet needs or expectations. This is not to say that administrators and counselors work less. It simply means that they have more control over their time. Even though emergencies occur in their roles/functions, they can shift the responsibility to another person or time slot. Therefore, they can plan quality time for professional growth activities. For this group of educators, time is a resource.

What makes this feasible is that administrators and counselors using quality time for professional growth (training/retraining) does not increase instructional costs to the schools. If a principal or superintendent attends a meeting outside the school campus, perhaps all day or even longer, no substitute is hired. The only cost to the school is registration and personal expenses.

Teachers, however, require substitutes when they are involved in training/retraining during school hours. Therefore, time is not a resource in the vital area of training/retraining. Money—another resource—must be expended for substitutes. Since substitute teachers are not considered by most schools to be a regular part of the faculty, funds for their support do not make a significant contribution to total quality.

To increase the commitment to time as a resource, schools could employ additional teachers at elementary grade levels and by subject area in the high school. These additional teachers would be a part of the regular faculty and would make a contribution to total quality. By having a staff that could handle the regular instructional program without committing all the teachers to classroom instruction, the school could implement training/retraining during quality time.

A second alternative, perhaps the most feasible and economical, is to hire teachers based on a contract year that goes beyond the student attendance calendar. This approach eliminates the problem of teachers being out of class, but still addresses the question of the need for teachers to have quality time for training and retraining.

Good training programs will concentrate on raising knowledge about real problems, followed by immediate application. The program will also make sure that by having teachers teaching teachers, the school is not compounding the mistakes currently being made. To do this, the school must know which teachers are competent in both knowledge and skill application, and utilize these competent teachers as mentors in the teacher entry year programs.

Deming Point 7—Institute Leadership

The aim of leadership should be to help teachers and students to do a better job. Leadership in management is in need of overhaul, as is the leadership of teachers.

Quality leadership will be required to implement continuous improvement in the educational program. This leadership will be based on the following characteristics:

- decisions based on data, not guesswork
- a scientific approach to the educational process
- focus on improving services and products, by improving how work gets done instead of just what is done

New relationships between administrators and teachers and teachers and students must be created and maintained. Administrator roles will be to help teachers and students do the best job possible, foreseeing and eliminating barriers that prevent teachers and students from doing quality work.

Also, administrators will need to make better use of teachers' knowledge in planning, monitoring, and evaluating the school's quality.

The Joiner Triangle[26] shown in Figure 8.1 symbolizes the relationship that quality, a scientific approach, and a feeling of being "all one team" must have if a school organization is to be successful. Taken together, these three elements are extremely stable and powerful.

One corner represents quality (of the educational program) as defined by the clients (students, parents, and community), for that is where the new focus must be. A second corner represents the scientific or data-based approach to studying the educational process, a strategy that leads to long-lasting fundamental improvement. The third corner represents employees and board working together as all one team to learn how to apply the principles needed to accomplish educational program quality control.

Two of the corners of the triangle are currently missing from many school organizations, thereby making the third corner (quality) impossible to achieve. Schools are still making too many educational decisions based on "hunches," or on tradition or insufficient data. Secondly, instead of being all one team, many school organizations are better characterized by the adversarial relationships that exist. Some of these conflicts can include teachers' unions vs. the administration, teachers' unions vs. the board, upper management vs. lower management, the board vs. the administration, the public vs. the administration, and the public vs. the board.

Despite all the reasons that it will be difficult to eliminate these adversarial relationships and create all one team, we must do it. This is the basic reason that American corporations and institutions are failing compared to foreign competition. The private sector of this nation has recognized this and begun to take steps to create the concept of being all one team. Education must do the same. Until we do so, we will be condemned to the continued measurement of quantity, and the evaluation that results from it.

[26]Scholtes, P. R. et al. 1989. *The Team Handbook, How to Use Teams to Improve Quality.* Madison, WI: Joiner Associates, Inc., pp. 1–4.

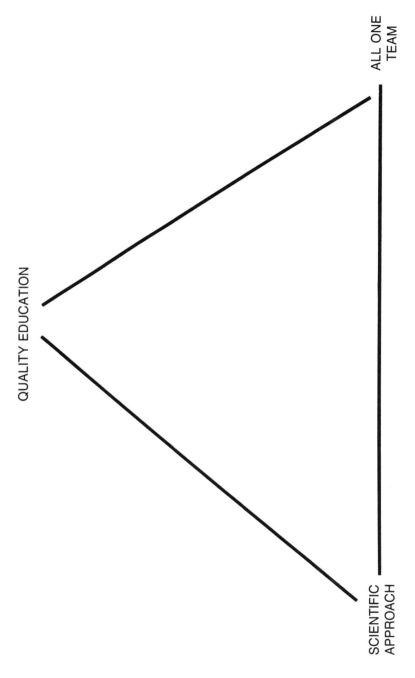

Figure 8.1 *A perspective on the future of educational leadership (reprinted from* The Team Handbook).

Mobility of Top Management

Job hopping among superintendents is as common in schools as it is in business and industry. The constant mobility of executives from one organization (school) to another creates prima donnas geared to quick results. The average superintendent reign in the United States for a school system is around three years. That isn't long enough for the quality approach that is being used in industry today to work effectively. If schools were to adopt industrial quality systems, they would have to deal with this problem.

This is another one of those problems that educators may have trouble solving alone. The problem does not lie totally with the mobile superintendent constantly trying to build up his/her *vitae*. Boards, often in the exercise of political agendas, constantly change superintendents of their own volition through buy-out, nonrenewal of contracts, or by political force.

So if this deadly disease is going to be eradicated by schools, boards of education are going to have to buy into the notion that stability at the top is needed for quality schools, and superintendents are going to have to buy into the concept also. It is difficult to conceive a strategy that could accomplish this on a wide scale. However, since it is becoming a part of the quality strategies of many industries, there is no reason to believe that boards of education could not be converted to this way of thinking. Perhaps now that education is considered to be in as much of a crisis as industry, this situation has the potential to be addressed.

Certainly, superintendents could adopt this philosophy with a simple change in career planning. An attitude adjustment would also help. But the attitude adjustment must involve not only administrators, but also boards and communities. If a state of stability, rather than mobility, is to occur in education, then a mindset, equating stability with the potential for quality and mobility with personal agendas and short-term results, must surface in the educational community.

Some Realities about Training Upper Management for Educational Program Total Quality

Experience with training upper level educational management (superintendents, assistant superintendents, central office specialists, and principals) points to some commonalities of their behavior. Upper school management:

- prefer to sit in training meetings that are attended exclusively by upper managers
- are reluctant to accept training from their subordinates
- are willing to be trained by outsiders who have earned public status through expertise
- listen eagerly to the experiences of upper managers of well-managed schools, especially the superintendents of such schools
- prefer a training site away from the office, for example, "retreats at a lodge"
- are willing to visit schools that have earned recognition through a quality program

This behavioral pattern offers guidelines to those who have the responsibility to plan meetings in which upper management are the trainees.

Deming Point 8—Drive Out Fear

Fear and anxiety are present at all levels of most schools. These feelings result from management's efforts to spur better performance from teachers and principals with the use of numerical goals, ranking, incentives, and slogans intended to stimulate the competitive spirit. The response to this fear and anxiety is defensiveness. By ridding schools of these old-style management techniques, the fear will be greatly reduced.

Some rating scales are self-imposed and some are imposed by state laws or educational standards. Some are more serious problems for schools than others.

One of the most harmful is evaluation of teacher performance, also called merit rating or annual review. Deming refers to this practice as "management by fear." He also states that it undermines teamwork, a concept that runs throughout his philosophy of quality.

Most states require that a written performance rating be filed on every teacher and administrator. Schools have augmented this with practices that establish individual objectives or targets, which form the basis for the evaluation. Therefore, even if schools were willing to try the Deming approach of eliminating ratings, they would have to get an exemption from state law and standards to do so. Of all of the Deming strategies that I have studied, this is the only one that could not be implemented by schools completely on their own initiative.

Even if a state law exemption is secured, in many districts, negotiated agreements with teachers' organizations and unions would still prevent abandonment of this practice unless the abandonment is negotiated.

Deming Point 9—Break Down Departmental Barriers

For schools, this point should include elimination of the barriers between buildings as well as departments. The educational infrastructure in most school districts includes multiple buildings. Therefore, the existence of barriers between and among buildings is an acute problem.

There is an old saying in educational circles that if you ask a high school teacher why the students are not learning up to expectations, he/she will blame the middle school. If you ask the middle school teacher, he/she will blame the elementary school. The elementary school teachers, having no teachers below them in the curriculum, will blame the parents.

There is a reason for this buck-passing. The teachers of the different levels do not jointly plan or problem solve. They are also not informed about the missions and operations of the other levels. The barriers naturally arise.

The barriers in schools are both horizontal and vertical. The horizontal barriers are most prevalent in the high schools, and are erected between departments such as English and math. Teachers in various departments tend to think within the confines of their own disciplines. Let me share a story to illustrate the department thinking mode.

This story involves proficiency tests. Students must demonstrate a certain level of achievement in the proficiency tests in order to graduate from high school. In this instance, the test results had just come in from the state department of education. The principal notified the teachers that the results were available for their perusal. An English teacher came into the office and asked to see the results. The principal handed him the overall results, which included English, math, and citizenship. The teacher informed the principal that he was only interested in the English results, since they were the only tests that affected him.

Thinking departmentally, the teacher is right. Thinking systematically, the teacher is wrong. If the test results in math and citizenship are poor, the school is going to have to apply more resources to these subject areas in order to improve the test results and graduation rates. It could be that the resources will be taken from the English department. Departmental thinking is only valid if one assumes that the rest of the system is not affected by what occurs in a particular department. But the system is almost always affected by the actions of the departments that make it up. Therefore, the more that departmental barriers are removed, the more systematic decision making can take place.

Vertical barriers occur grade to grade and course to course when prerequisites are present. Perhaps the most significant vertical barrier is building to building. There is something about the physical separation of people that increases the barriers.

The key to breaking down the departmental barriers are the establishment of K–12 curriculum development and K–12 staff development. Neither of these organizational processes should be strictly building enterprises. They should be planned and implemented at the system level. By developing curriculum from a K–12 perspective and by planning and implementing staff development from the total district perspective, the school system can create the communication links and decision-making processes necessary to breakdown departmental barriers.

Lots of school districts are already approaching curriculum and staff development from a district perspective. One additional step may be necessary to convert from a traditional to a quality model. The sequence of curriculum development needs to be reversed. Instead of starting at the primary level and progressing through high school, curriculum development should start at the high school level and progress backward through the middle school and then to the elementary school and primary level. The rationale for this switch is that the internal quality question, "What can I do to make your job more effective?" is best answered by asking the client upward in the school graded structure. The high school would ask the colleges and workplaces. Middle schools would ask the high schools. Elementary schools would ask the middle schools. Parents of preschoolers would ask the elementary schools.

This quality question could best be answered through curriculum development. Therefore, the curriculum development process should start with the high school design based on client needs and proceed back to the kindergarten level. Otherwise, it is not client-based, and thus is not a quality approach.

Personnel switches between buildings and departments must occur so that people can learn about the problems others have. The school system must have common goals, and its members must work as a team to solve problems, set policies, and map out new directions. The most important thing to remember is that people who are forced to administer policies that they had no hand in drafting or with which they disagree will do so halfheartedly and without uniformity.

Deming Point 10—Eliminate Slogans, Targets, and Exhortations

School administrators intend that slogans, exhortations, and numerical targets will motivate teachers to work harder in competition with themselves or others. Standards and management by objectives (MBO) are traditionally assumed to produce better performance. These slogans, exhortations, and numerical targets are all extrinsic motivators—rewards or punishments—intended to urge people to higher attainment. They are barriers to intrinsic motivation, a pillar of total quality management philosophy.

Eliminate slogans calling for pride or new levels of teacher effort. Such exhortations only create adversary relationships, as most of the causes of low quality and low productivity belong to the system and thus lie beyond the power of the teachers and the other workforce personnel.

Slogans only generate frustration and resentment. They are based on the supposition that employees could, if they tried, do better. Teachers perceive slogans and exhortations as signals that management not only doesn't understand their problems, but it doesn't care enough to find out about them. It is totally impossible for anyone or any group to perform outside a stable system, either above or below it. Total quality management will create a stable system, and eliminate the need for slogans and other exhortations that fall on deaf ears.

Deming Point 11—Eliminate Numerical Quotas

Statistical process control, as operationally defined in this text, is not congruent with management based on numerical quotas. The setting of goals and evaluating both goals and people by quantifiable output are contradictory to the total quality management concepts of identifying stable systems and then working with continuous improvement. Here are some specific examples of problems caused by numerical quotas.

Goals Are Often Arbitrarily Set

Many states are implementing proficiency tests that a student must pass before they are issued a high school diploma. A school I am familiar with decided that their goal was to have 95 percent of their students pass this proficiency test on the first try. I asked the superintendent how they decided on that number. He said that the curriculum council of teachers and board members decided that it was achievable.

The problem with this approach is that it does not take into account information from the current system. The questions that the school should have been asking itself are: What percent are passing on the first try now? Is it 95 percent? If not, why not? What are we going to do differently this year? Why are we only aiming for 95 percent? To use total quality management principles, the focus should be on using data to create control limits, to assess the educational processes, to improve the processes based on what the system is currently producing, and to work toward continuous improvement.

If the educational processes are stable, then there is no value in setting a goal. You will get what the system will deliver and no more. If you want to improve, study the processes within the system and make adjustments. If the educational processes are not stable, there is no point in setting a goal; it can't be reached. If it was, you couldn't measure it anyway. If you did, you wouldn't know why because the system is unstable, therefore, you don't know if the variation is common or special. So the goal is pointless and valueless. Focus on the outcome will not improve the system's processes or activities.

Setting Quotas Leads to Marginal Work

The quota becomes the goal—high for a few, average for many, and low for a few. The teacher focuses on getting as many as possible to achieve the quota. She will tend to disregard, or give less emphasis to, the students who are either already above the quota or have little chance of achieving the quota. This practice means that the average students will receive the most resources, time, and energy, while the extremes away from the average are left to swim or sink on their own.

What is lost in this process is the pursuit of quality and the intrinsic desire to continuously improve.

Quotas Do Not Take into Account the Differences in People, Specifically Teachers

Variation in their performance is natural and unavoidable. It is a common cause, not a special cause. One-half of the teachers will always, by definition of a norm-referenced system, perform below the mean. It is not management's job to tell this half that they are performing below the average. It is also counterproductive to try to get these teachers to do better if they are performing within the system.

Management's job is to improve everyone's performance through training and education, and to improve the system. Management should also identify those teachers who represent a special cause of variation, try to help them, and if unsuccessful, act accordingly to create a stable system.

Deming Point 12—Remove Barriers to Worker Pride

We must remove barriers that rob the teachers of their right to pride of workmanship. This means abolishment of the annual or merit rating scheme and of management by objective. Listen to the teachers, and have clear expectations over time. Give them ongoing feedback on work, institute and maintain training/retraining, and do not evaluate critically without suggestions. Make effectiveness, not efficiency, the goal of administration.

To utilize teacher expertise and increase teacher pride, the administrator must overcome certain inherent biases that may be present. They are:

(1) An atmosphere of blame—If present, it always inhibits the free flow of communications.
(2) The supervisor/subordinate relationship—The fact that the boss asks the question tends to influence the answer the subordinate gives.

(3) Conflict in loyalties—Teachers may be wary of communicating information that might create problems for their colleagues, the union, or someone else.

Overcoming such biases requires the use of special skills in data collection and analysis. A case study will help clarify these needed skills.

In a school system, a joint committee of administrators and teachers held regular meetings to discuss educational program quality. At one meeting, an intermediate teacher complained that the fifth graders could not do addition with carrying. The curriculum director answered by saying, "The primary teachers know they are supposed to teach this math skill. I'll tell them again that they aren't getting this across." In two sentences, he/she managed to invoke three biases:

(1) He/she created an atmosphere of blame: "It's the primary teachers' fault."

(2) He/she cut off further discussion of a genuine problem by "pulling rank," that is, using his status as boss. The implication was, "Don't bring that up again."

(3) He/she made an intermediate teacher feel that to open his/her mouth further would be to make more trouble for the primary teachers.

That was a remarkable negative accomplishment, considering that the school climate was sufficiently informal to support such a promising meeting in the first place.

When someone with more skill looked into the matter with a scientific eye, the problem was found to be in the curriculum, which had neglected to note that addition with carrying was to be taught in the primary grades.

Too many people are blaming the failures of American education on teachers. The last thing teachers need is to hear this same charge of incompetence from their own administrators. What teachers really need is an ally—someone to defend them, and to make them feel that they are a valued part of the total quality management team.

Deming Point 13—Institute Education/Self-Improvement

It is not enough to have good people in your organization. Employees must be continually acquiring new knowledge and skills in methods.

This program of education must fit people into ever-changing jobs and responsibilities.

How will school employees believe that their organization is constantly improving unless they can see that they themselves are constantly improving? Remember that education is a service industry, operated not by machines but by people. No improvement in technology or infrastructure is more important than improvement in the people who make up the school.

The most fascinating feedback from the primary research for this book concerned profound knowledge. Consistently, the quality representatives who were interviewed claimed that one of the major weaknesses of their total quality effort was that their companies spent too much time on strategies and not enough time studying the implications of knowledge on total quality management.

Where knowledge is of particular significance to total quality management is in the education/improvement component. Within this component is the need to understand and apply adult learning theory. Any organization that attempts to raise the level of knowledge will be doing so with adult learners. Therefore, a knowledge of adult learning processes is a prerequisite to the increase of profound knowledge in the organization.

There are many accepted principles of adult learning. The following are vital to any school working toward total quality management.

- Once convinced that a change is certain, adults will engage in any learning that will help them cope with the transformation.
- For most adults, learning is its own reward.
- Increasing one's self-esteem is a strong motivator for engaging in learning experiences.
- There are "teachable moments" in the lives of adults.
- Wisdom is a separate intellectual function that develops as people grow older.
- Adults prefer single-concept, single-theory learning experiences.
- Information that conflicts sharply with what is already held to be true is integrated more slowly.
- Fast-paced, complex, or unusual learning tasks interfere with the concepts they are intended to teach or illustrate.
- Adults tend to take errors more personally and are less willing to take more risks.

- Adults prefer self-directed and self-designed projects over group learning experiences.
- Adults prefer face-to-face, one-to-one access to experts.
- A trainer of adults needs to take an eclectic approach in developing strategies and procedures.
- As they get older, adults can still learn new things.

As schools work with their employees in the pursuit of constant self-improvement, they should follow the principles of adult learning. To avoid doing so will seriously jeopardize the chances of success. Take the time to know the psychological aspects of profound knowledge before moving on to strategies and procedures leading to total quality management.

Deming Point 14—Putting Everyone to Work, to Realize the Transformation

Put everybody in the school system to work to accomplish the transformation to total quality management in education. The transformation is everybody's job.

The transformation process will take team management and initiative from top management. However, every employee will be involved in quality. Top management must agree on the meaning of the fourteen points just discussed, and top management must also have the courage to feel dissatisfaction with past performance and to pursue change. Management, at all levels, must explain the fourteen points to the students and teachers. And most important of all, every activity must be treated as a process.

The most frequent cause of failure in any quality improvement effort is the lack of involvement or a sense of indifference on the part of top and middle management. Therefore, the active leadership and participation of administrators, beginning at the top, is essential.

Quality cannot be delegated to others. Administrators must lead the transformation effort to ensure long-lasting success. They must become leaders instead of bosses, coaches instead of enforcers. They must change their focus from blaming and controlling individuals to preventing and eliminating problems. They must learn new skills and approaches for stabilizing and improving the process. They must understand variation and know how to use data effectively.

Don't try to correct all the quality problems at once. Go slowly, and be thorough. The multi-year strategy addresses these questions:

- Which quality projects have the best chance of immediate success?
- What resources, financial and personnel, will be needed to sustain initial education, training, and quality projects? Who will provide guidance and technical assistance to administrators, supervisors, teachers, and project teams?
- Who will coordinate logistics, details, and school system wide communication?

Early efforts toward educational program quality should be projects that involve teams of people that have a good chance of success. Projects that are too large or diffuse can cause frustration and dampen the enthusiasm for the continual effort toward quality.

With an eye to the long term, and with commitment to the new management philosophy on the part of everyone involved, total quality management can be implemented in schools, providing the same successes for American education that it provided for American industry.

QUALITY CHARACTERISTIC 15—THE 85/15 RULE

To accept the 85/15 rule means that schools, especially administrations, must adopt a new attitude toward teachers and teachers' unions. There is a lot of "if we could only get the teachers to do this" attitude. School management also has the attitude that the curriculum and the testing programs are well designed, but that there is a weakness in the instructional program. The belief is that the management-controlled systems (curriculum and testing) are in place, and that any weakness therefore lies in the teaching, which is not perceived as controlled by the administration.

Following industry's lead, schools should look at organizational breakdowns instead of looking at individual teachers when trying to improve the overall system of quality.

If schools accepted the 85/15 rule, they would look at the following organizational components:

(1) The content and methodology match between curriculum and assessment/testing

(2) The content and methodology match between textbooks and planned curriculum documents

(3) The soundness and viability of curriculum content

(4) The organizational focus and constancy with regard to teacher and student academic behavior

(5) The appropriateness of their teachers' training and a staff development program based on this assessment

(6) A staff development program based on the identified organizational weaknesses and failures

The 85/15 rule also means disavowing a number of prominent managerial myths in schools. These perceptions have been extensive, and have led many school administrators astray. They must be put to rest if educational total quality is the goal.

(1) The teaching staff is mainly responsible for the school's problems. (Reality—Leadership is responsible for 80 to 90 percent.)

(2) Teachers could do good quality work, but they lack the motivation. (Reality—Teachers need to be empowered.)

(3) Quality will get top priority if upper management so decrees. (Reality—It will not happen without fundamental changes.)

(4) To change people's behavior, it is first necessary to change their attitude. (Reality—It is the other way around.)

In the past, too much blame has been placed on teachers, and not enough blame has been placed on the current structure of America's schools. When school leaders come to accept that 85 percent of the problems of education are due to organizational structure, and only 15 percent to personnel, they will be able to take concrete action toward changing this structure. Only in this way will it be possible to implement a program of total quality management in schools.

QUALITY CHARACTERISTIC 16—QUALITY AS A PEOPLE ISSUE

Industry's definition of quality based on customer satisfaction and continuous improvement fits well with education. In view of the elusive nature of quality in educational circles, this definition is defensible and reasonable. Currently, educational definitions of quality center mainly around standardized test scores. Schools would be better served by using the industrial definition of quality based on the two criteria just presented. Education is a human endeavor. Measuring human beings in an absolute sense has always been hard, but measuring continuous improvement is not difficult. It also erases the problems relating to differing abilities and potential. Even the worst of the human race can improve. And of course, the standard of customer satisfaction foregoes all the formal measures and gets to the issue of how well people perceive your efforts. Over a period of time, quality is recognizable to the public. If you can get taxpayers to keep sending their children to you, that is an indication that your school is a quality school; if you can't, it is an indication of the opposite. This is a new way to look at the profession of education. But just hanging out a shingle does not insure a doctor that he/she will have patients. Over a period of time, the doctor must demonstrate quality work. Let it be so with teaching.

Quality cannot be a people issue in the schools so long as teaching is an isolated activity and anything else that a teacher does is "extracurricular." Education must rid itself of the "extracurricular syndrome" to achieve the quality approach.

In industry, total quality approaches are feasible and working because training, group efforts, and personal growth efforts are done as a part of the regular workday. Natural work groups function during the workday.

In education, total quality approaches will not work so long as personal development is extracurricular. It is impossible to achieve the personal development required for a total quality movement so long as the natural work group of teachers consists of one teacher, isolated except for department- or grade-level meetings, with the natural work activity being teaching only.

Special work groups currently meet after school for less than professional wages, or irregularly during school and for a period of time too short to have significant impact. Additional teaching staff would be required to have natural work groups. The money will be found by having more teachers with more responsibility, and fewer administrators with less teacher supervisory responsibility.

QUALITY CHARACTERISTIC 17—EMPLOYEE SUGGESTION PROGRAM

This industrial characteristic is easily adaptable to schools. It is a prelude to the teacher empowerment process already underway in many schools. The idea also represents the whole change in management philosophy proposed by total quality management, which accepts that people doing the work usually know more about the work than the people supervising the work.

Schools will have the same cultural problem with participation that industry has experienced. However, due to the high level of formal education required to be a teacher, the potential for increased participation on the part of the teachers is good.

SUMMARY

This chapter has examined the final four quality characteristics—the change in management philosophy, the 85/15 rule, quality as a people issue, and an employee suggestion program. In particular, the new philosophy of management focuses on the fourteen points put forward by W. Edwards Deming, the world's leading authority on total quality management. All of these quality characteristics stress that teachers are generally very skilled and competent, and that the problems in American education—like those in American industry—lie primarily in the way the organizations are structured and run. It will do us no good to continue blaming teachers for America's decline, or to attempt to motivate them through puerile slogans or numerical quotas.

What we need to do is to treat teachers as professionals, listen to their suggestions, and encourage them to engage in constant self-improvement. With this new attitude, and with the other elements of the new management philosophy, it will be possible to break down the barriers within school organizations so that all employees will be part of one team, dedicated to the constant pursuit of educational quality.

Putting Total Quality Management to Work in Schools

More than anything else, total quality management represents a change in philosophy. Philosophy is a way of thinking. Change is a process. Therefore, the school system that adopts total quality management must address and cope with a new philosophy while simultaneously grappling with the difficulties associated with any significant change.

Perhaps as significant as what a school system must do in adopting total quality management is what it must not do. Specifically, it must not treat total quality management as a change involving many unconnected strategies, each of which can stand on its own.

To implement total quality management, a school system must change the way it views schools, and it must be willing to challenge some of the beliefs upon which school management has been based for decades. A good way to do this is to change the paradigm.

WHAT ARE PARADIGMS?

Paradigms are models or patterns of thinking and behaving. They create the rules and regulations and establish the standards that define success within a field. Problems are solved within the boundaries of these paradigms.

However, paradigms oftentimes keep people from accepting new ideas. There is a tendency for people to adjust data and information by filtering it through scientific mindsets that agree with their paradigms. Therefore, data or information that agrees with the current paradigms is more likely to gain acceptance than data that disagrees with the current paradigm. This is called the "paradigm effect,"[27] which tends to

[27]Barker, J. A. 1990. "Discovering the Future, the Business of Paradigms," a videotape. Burnsville, MN: Chart House Learning Corporation.

blind people and organizations to new opportunities. It causes them to try to discover the future through the current paradigm. This, of course, limits peoples' thinking.

For school systems to give total quality management a chance to succeed, school leadership must be willing to look at new paradigms relative to school purpose and management philosophy. This is, of course, risky, because all the data supports the current paradigm. Therefore, in order to be a "paradigm pioneer," a person must be willing to change without recourse to the "safe" data base. School systems that refuse to look at total quality management until the research says that it works will have to wait a while, because currently there is not enough data and information to unequivocally support total quality management in education (though industry is a different story). The reason is that the data does not fit the current educational management paradigm. School leaders who implement total quality management will do so because they believe the current school management paradigms are wrong.

Paradigms are common, even though they may not be identified as such by the people using them. Since they are models or patterns of thinking and behaving, they can be identified through observation. The people using them will tell you what they believe or do. Those beliefs and actions constitute the paradigms, even if the people in question do not define them as their paradigms.

They are useful as long as they are "a" paradigm and not "the" paradigm. People who can only see their own paradigm are said to be suffering from "paradigm paralysis."[27] They are limited in their ability to see the future. Therefore, they are limited in their ability to work toward continuous improvement.

People who create new paradigms tend to be from outside the organization or field. Bureaucracies and structures with an interest in the status quo tend to oppose fundamental change within their organization or field. Such bureaucracies are often powerful enough to keep change from happening within the organization.

This is an accurate description of the current state of affairs in education. Forces from outside the schools such as the federal and state governments, business and industry, and a significant part of the general public, are demanding that education change its paradigms. Most of the school reform of the 1980s and 1990s has originated outside the educational structure. This book, though written by someone within the educational structure, is asking the educational community to consider a concept—total quality management—that originated in business and industry. This should not be viewed as unusual, since change from the outside is a common occurrence in the culture.

New rules or boundaries are always "written on the edge." In most cases, the scientific evidence does not support the new rules because the new rules do not fit the existing paradigm. Practitioners who adopt total quality management must be courageous enough to accept that schools are enough like private enterprise for total quality management to work in schools, even though evidence may not yet exist to support the new paradigm in the early stages. Remember, paradigm pioneers must have great courage and trust in their own judgment until such time as the paradigm shifts and the new data is accepted.

People can choose to shed old paradigms for new ones. Paradigms don't change unless people change them. Paradigm switches do not occur through automatic evolutionary processes. They switch due to the efforts of people.

When paradigm shifts do occur, an interesting phenomenon takes place—everyone goes back to zero. When the rules change, past guarantees or successes mean nothing for the future. There is a new playing field. The old data is no longer relevant, and new data is now acceptable. This fact is alarming to school systems that are currently considered excellent. If the paradigm shifts, their status as excellent school systems is threatened. On the other hand, school systems that have not been considered successful under the existing paradigm will get a fresh start when the paradigm shifts.

The key to knowing when to lead a paradigm shift involves good research and development to increase knowledge needed for predictability. If a school system successful under the current paradigm does not attempt to predict the future needs of its clients and be proactive in meeting them, it runs the risk of being left behind when the shift occurs.

Let's look at a couple of examples to illustrate the need to be ready to include predictability as a necessary component of school leadership. The companies who made carburetors in the early 1980s were making the best quality carburetors in the history of the industry. The price was within the price range of the customers. Despite this, they still went out of business when fuel injection was developed and accepted. The carburetor manufacturers had not worked with predictability. Swiss watchmakers made the best watches in the world in 1960. In fact, they had 80 percent of the world market and 90 percent of the world's profits from watch manufacturing. Today, Japan leads the world in watchmaking. Why? Because the Swiss refused to see and adjust to a paradigm shift in the late 1960s. The quartz watch, invented by the Swiss themselves, was developed and sold by Seiko of Japan and Texas Instruments of the United States and became the new paradigm of watch design.

Why did the Swiss ignore their own invention? Because they were judging it by their old paradigm. The quartz design did not have a mainspring or the other parts of the old watch paradigm. Why did the carburetor manufacturers not see the future of fuel injection? Because fuel injection did not involve a carburetor, and cars had to have a carburetor. Right? No! Wrong. Cars only have to have a way to start the engine. The design is insignificant. The function is what is necessary.

A part of school management must be involved with predictability, so that educators can discover the future and avoid being left behind by the times.

THE CURRENT EDUCATIONAL MANAGEMENT PARADIGM

The current educational management paradigm emphasizes hierarchical order, superordinate/subordinate function, control, command, up to down communication, division of labor, delegation, authority, job descriptions, and individual responsibility.

An interesting way to look at this paradigm is to ask the question, "What changes that can't be made today within the thinking of this paradigm would fundamentally change what you are doing?" The answer to this question will reveal the paradigm shift needed in order for a school system to pursue the concept of total quality management as currently defined by the literature and practice of private business and industry.

THE TOTAL QUALITY MANAGEMENT PARADIGM

The total quality management paradigm emphasizes the client priority, the lack of hierarchy, self monitoring and inspection, collaboration, horizontal communication, cooperation, flow charts, and team responsibility.

This new paradigm involves many facets, that, when taken collectively, represent the changes in philosophy that are needed for a school system to implement total quality management.

Some of the paradigm shifts from current school management to total quality management are:

(1) From organization-driven control to client-driven control

(2) From fixed standards to continuous improvement

(3) From educational quality defined by goals and objectives to educational quality defined by the client

(4) From national comparison to international comparison

(5) From lockstep work process to wholistic work process

(6) From geographical monopoly/control over educational clients to client satisfaction based on more parental choice

(7) From emphasis on personnel appraisal to personal development plans for all administrators and teachers

(8) From vertical work flow to horizontal work flow

(9) From providing information to the public to gathering information from the public

(10) From the specialization approach to curriculum, staff development, and administration to an integrated systems approach

(11) From individual process systems to team process systems

(12) From hierarchical control to total involvement

(13) From isolation to collaboration in teaching

(14) From pipeline to cyclical management

(15) From quality control through external inspection to quality design and self inspection

(16) From organizational expectations to client expectations

(17) From educational quality based on internal definitions to educational quality based on client satisfaction

(18) From problem solving to continuous improvement

(19) From control and command to commitment and teamwork

(20) From public relations to public surveying

(21) From emphasis on additional resources to emphasis on the reallocation of resources

(22) From expansionist thinking to abandonment thinking

(23) From delegation to abandonment

(24) From support personnel to self-supporting systems (less supervisors and more teachers)

(25) From supervisory inspection to self inspection

(26) From judgments by school officials about public perceptions to the acceptance of public perceptions as a reality that must be addressed by the educational community

(27) From accountability meaning minimum standards through the use of proficiency tests for graduation, to accountability meaning continuous improvements measured by test data over a period of years

(28) From organizational renewal through recruitment of new personnel to renewal through retention and training/retraining (reward teachers and administrators for staying in one school system)

(29) From the natural work function of teachers consisting of teaching only, to a teacher work function that includes overall school quality, i.e., curriculum, instruction, and staff development

(30) From individual job knowledge as sufficient to organizational knowledge as a necessity (teachers must know what other teachers do so they can ask and respond to the internal quality question—"How can I help you do your job better?"—the same principle would hold true for administrators)

(31) From leadership demanding educational quality to leadership behavior that role models quality

Once the knowledge of what total quality management means has been achieved, the school system is ready to proceed to the next step in putting total quality management to work. That step involves gaining the appropriate level of acceptance within the school culture that makes the total quality management effort feasible.

GAINING ACCEPTANCE OF TOTAL QUALITY MANAGEMENT

Three groups must be supportive of total quality management for it to be a feasible approach. These groups are the board of education, the administrators, and the teachers' union or organization. If there is no teachers' union, then the teachers as a group must be supportive.

The changes that total quality management will make in the way that the schools do business are so massive that to attempt to implement total quality management without the board being a major player is impossible. The board must be fully informed about what the concept means and how it works. No school should make the attempt to implement total quality management without board approval. This is the first political step in the process. If support is not forthcoming, the administrator should continue to communicate with the board until such time as the board decides to initiate and support the process. If that support never develops, then total quality management should not be initiated.

Middle management loses more power than any other group with the advent of total quality management. Most of the paradigm shifts discussed at the beginning of this chapter directly change the role of middle management. In essence, middle management, supervisors, central office administrators and coordinators, principals, and assistant principals will become more like facilitators, resource persons, and servitors for their internal clients. This role shift will not be successful unless it is made willingly. Middle management works directly with the two groups who ultimately decide the success of all educational programs—the teachers and the students. Therefore, middle management is the only sector of the administration that works directly at the operations level. Either they buy in, or the total quality management style will not get off the ground.

The biggest change that total quality management brings to middle management is that positions move from being authority-based to being expertise-based. The only way total quality management can be successful is if middle management personnel are experts in the processes of total quality management. To attempt the transformation with authoritarians will fail. To attempt the transformation with authoritarians falsely presenting themselves as experts will also fail. The process must be led by middle management with the knowledge to understand and lead the transformation.

In working with teachers, keep in mind the following things.

(1) Do not let the adversarial relationships caused by collective bargaining destroy the "all one team" concept discussed in previous chapters.

(2) Take a positive approach. Do not assume that teachers will oppose total quality management. Assume that all teachers are good

people who will support any movement by management that they think will help them teach better and help their students to learn better.

(3) Don't initiate total quality management to undermine or destroy the union. Create a partnership with the union. Teachers and therefore teachers' unions know that the current adversarial relationship between management and teachers is not productive. They also know that the public is demanding different results from schools, and they are aware that they must participate in any significant improvement effort.

(4) Expect the unions to stumble at first. They must also undergo a transformation within their own organization before they can participate in total quality management.

Initiate Training/Retraining

It is vital that training/retraining occurs before reorganizing for total quality management. It does no good to reorganize if everyone is going to act the same as they did before. Do the training first so that the change will be a behavioral change, not just a title change.

This phase of implementation could be short term or long term. It all depends on how much behavioral change and expertise development is needed. When you decide how long to spend on training, remember that until this phase is completed there can be no total quality management.

Reorganize for Total Quality

To implement total quality management, the school will reorganize resources and roles. The reorganizing of these two areas will automatically result in a flattening of the hierarchy. The key is that the reorganizing is based on the functions that have been described in all the chapters as necessary components of total quality management.

Collect Baseline Data

Since total quality management is based on continuous improvement, the school should identify all the areas, instructional or noninstructional, in which they are going to strive for continuous improvement. Then they should establish the baseline data upon which to collect and compare data to measure continuous improvement.

Put Everybody to Work to Accomplish the Transformation

If all the steps explained in this chapter so far have been achieved, the school is now ready to put total quality management into operation. The next step is to plan for action. Enough people in the school must understand the process and the transformation needed or leadership is helpless. The change must involve everyone in the school.

This chapter could be summed up in the following questions that a school system should ask itself as it begins implementing total quality management. The answers to all the questions must be yes. If the school cannot answer all of the questions with yes, then it must pause, communicate, and learn until it is comfortable with a yes answer for the question.

The questions, in order of consideration are:

(1) Does the school leadership accept the new total quality management paradigm?
(2) Has total quality management as a philosophy of management gained acceptance from the board of education, the administration, and the teachers' union?
(3) Has the training and retraining that is needed to accomplish the knowledge and attitudinal change necessary for total quality management been completed?
(4) Has the school been reorganized to create the resources and roles for total quality management?
(5) Has the baseline data that will be used to measure continuous improvement been collected and presented?
(6) Is everyone in the school system involved in the transformation to total quality management?
(7) Does the school have a plan of action?

ASSUMPTIONS OF A CLIENT-FOCUSED SCHOOL

In addition to making the paradigm shifts presented in this chapter, the school that wishes to implement total quality management needs to embrace the following assumptions.

(1) Trying to improve schools within the current process and teaching methods will not correct the deficiencies in the organization. Instead, schools need training and new management tools, such as total quality management, to restructure schools.

(2) The new learning demand on schools will require that they develop networks and alliances with parents, other schools, the district office, business and industry, community agencies, and other institutions. These connections are essential to help current teachers master the strategies needed to make the learning process less passive for the learner.

(3) A school readiness program for both parents and children is essential to the transformation to client-centered schools.

(4) There needs to be a broad-based consensus with common operational definitions on what our students should know and how we will assess that they know it.

(5) Parents must be equal partners in their children's education. Early preschool intervention strategies such as preschool for three and four year olds, adequate health care and nutritional care, and parenting programs are provided.

(6) Frequent parent conferences and continuous student progress reports are essential in making parents active educational partners.

(7) The roles of the student and the teacher will be altered. The student becomes an actual rather than a passive learner, and the teacher facilitates the student learning as a resource person exhibiting coaching behavior.

(8) School will concentrate on creating and maintaining quality through continuous improvement. This will be pursued through training/retraining for teachers and administrators, integration of technology into the learning environment, restructuring the instructional program, and modifying the delivery system.

THE CHARACTERISTICS OF A CLIENT-FOCUSED SCHOOL SYSTEM

If the assumptions of the client-focused school system are accurate, such a school will possess the following characteristics:

- continuous total quality management principles
- cooperative learning strategies at all grade levels
- the instructional program restructured to meet world class standards
- ongoing inservice training for all personnel
- encouragement and support for innovation, field testing, piloting, and evaluating and adopting new ideas
- networking with parents, other community agencies, schools, and institutions
- operational definitions in everyday use
- school-based decision making and management design
- congruity among curriculum, instruction, and assessment (testing)
- common vision among clients, staff, and governance structure
- modifications to the instructional delivery system
- thinking and problem-solving skills throughout the curriculum
- use of appropriate technology in both management and instruction
- use of teaming both management and instruction
- student as an active learner, striving toward learning to be a learner
- teacher's role is coach/facilitator
- full-service support to student and parent
- long-term relationship developed with parents, students, and school venders
- parents are viewed as equal partners in the education of their child
- a client-oriented staff
- use of statistical process control in determining individual learning plans and assessments

CONCLUSION

This chapter has attempted to show that for total quality management to work for schools, a new paradigm is called for. This paradigm will create a new set of assumptions, which will, in turn, create a new set of characteristics.

These changes are consistent with the impetus for new initiatives in school reform. This impetus is based on the erosion in confidence, on the part of many business and political leaders, in the school's ability to keep our society economically and intellectually competitive in the world's economy.

Such a strong charge demands substantive action. Total quality management for schools is a daring departure from the past. Most assuredly, total quality management is not a new label for an old solution. It will require new philosophies, assumptions, theories, and strategies. That is what society is demanding. More importantly, that is what society needs.

APPENDIX

THE INTERVIEWS

The initial interview dates and the persons interviewed are listed in the chronological order of occurrence. All initial interviews were conducted in person. Many subsequent interviews, both in person, over the phone, and through the mail have occurred between these people and myself. In addition, these quality experts have referred me to other persons in quality both within and outside their companies. All of their input was considered and included in the identification of the characteristics of quality systems in private enterprise.

(1) George Dyson, Senior Staff Engineer, Engineering Statistical Division, General Electric Airplane Engines, One Neuman Way, Cincinnati, Ohio 45215. Date of interview—September 10, 1990.

(2) Mort Saylor, Corporate Director, Quality Standards and Certification, Cincinnati Milicron, 4701 Marburg Avenue, Cincinnati, Ohio 45209. Date of interview—December 14, 1990.

(3) Scott Kuhr, Quality Assurance Advisor, AT&T, Cincinnati, Ohio. Date of interview—December 20, 1990.

(4) Katie Wolfram, Director, Consumer Research, The Kroger Company, Cincinnati, Ohio. Date of interview—January 7, 1991.

(5) Terrence Russell, Manager, Continuous Improvement Operation, Aircraft Engines Engineering Division, GE Aircraft Engines, One Neuman Way, Cincinnati, Ohio 45215. Date of interview—January 10, 1991.

(6) Paul W. Robinson, Manager, Evendale Quality Training and Support, One Neuman Way, Cincinnati, Ohio 45215. Date of interview—January 30, 1991.

(7) Richard M. Glover, Vice President, Product Supply, Engineering, and Jean Kinney, Corporate Quality, Procter and Gamble Company, Two Procter and Gamble Plaza, Cincinnati, Ohio 45202. Date of interview—January 31, 1991.

(8) Ronald R. Monson, Transition Coordinator, Cincinnati Gas and Electric Company, P.O. Box 960, Cincinnati, Ohio 45201. Date of interview—February 11, 1991.

(9) James A. Miller, Manager, Quality Department, Ford Motor Company, Batavia Transmission Plant, 1981 Front Wheel Drive, Batavia, Ohio 45103. Date of interview—February 28, 1991.

(10) William Johnson, President and CEO, and Teri Johnson, Operations Manager, Robin Color Lab, Central Parkway, Cincinnati, Ohio. Date of interview—November 14, 1991.

BIBLIOGRAPHY

Banks, J. 1989. *Principles of Quality Control*. New York, NY: John Wiley and Sons.

Barker, J. 1990. "Discovering the Future, the Business of Paradigms," a videotape. Burnsville, MN: Chart House Learning Corporation.

Deming, W. E. "Videotapes: The Deming Library." Chicago, IL: Films Incorporation.

Deming, W. E. 1991. *Out of the Crisis*. Cambridge, MA: Massachusetts Institute of Technology, Center for Advanced Engineering Study.

Deming, W. E. 1991. *Quality, Productivity, and Competitive Position*. Los Angeles, CA: Quality Enhancement Seminars, Inc.

Dyson, G. Senior Staff Engineer, Engineering Statistical Division, General Electric Airplane Engines, Cincinnati, OH: Interview, September 10, 1990.

English, F. 1988. *Curriculum Auditing*. Lancaster, PA: Technomic Publishing Co., Inc.

Glasser, W. 1990. "The Quality School," *Phi Delta Kappan*, February.

Glover, R. Vice President, Product Supply, Engineering, Procter and Gamble Co., Cincinnati, OH: Interview January 11, 1991.

Grant, E. and R. Leavenworth. 1988. *Statistical Quality Control*. New York, NY: McGraw-Hill.

Halberstam, D. 1969. *The Reckoning*. New York, NY: Avon Books.

Herzberg, F. 1987. "One More Time: How Do You Motivate Employees?" *Harvard Business Review* (Sept./Oct.):109.

Inai, M. 1986. *Kaizer: The Key to Japan's Competitive Success*. New York, NY: McGraw-Hill.

Ishikawa, K. 1985. *What Is Total Quality Control? The Japanese Way*. Englewood Cliffs, NJ: Prentice-Hall, Inc.

Johnson, T. Operations Manager, Robin Color Lab, Cincinnati, OH: Interview, November 14, 1991.

Johnson, W. President and CEO, Robin Color Lab, Cincinnati, OH: Interview, November 14, 1991.

Joiner, B. and P. Scholter. 1985. "Total Leadership vs. Management by Control." Madison, WI: Joiner Associates, Inc.

Juran, J. M. 1988. *Juran on Planning for Quality*. New York, NY: The Free Press.

Juran, J. M. 1989. *Juran on Leadership for Quality*. New York, NY: The Free Press.

Juran, J. M. and F. M. Gryna, Jr. 1980. *Quality Planning and Analysis*. New York, NY: McGraw-Hill.

Kinney, J. Corporate Quality, Procter and Gamble, Cincinnati, OH: Interview, January 31, 1991.

Kuhr, S. Quality Assurance Advisor, American Telephone and Telegraph, Cincinnati, OH: Interview, December 20, 1990.

Kume, H. 1988. *Statistical Methods for Quality Improvement*. Tokyo, Japan: Association for Overseas Technical Scholarship.

Mann, N. R. 1989. *The Keys to Excellence*. Los Angeles, CA: Prestwick Books.

Martin, C. "Standardized Test Study," unpublished manuscript, Cincinnati, OH, 1990.

Miller, J. Manager, Quality Department, Ford Motor Company, Batavia Transmission Plant, Batavia, OH: Interview, February 28, 1991.

Moen, R. 1989. *The Deming Philosophy for Improving the Educational Process*. Cincinnati, OH: Associates in Process Improvement.

Monson, R. Transition Coordinator, Cincinnati Gas and Electric Company, Cincinnati, OH: Interview, February 11, 1991.

Peters, T. 1988. *Thriving on Chaos*. New York, NY: Alfred A. Knopf.

Robinson, P. W. Manager, Evendale Quality Training and Support, Cincinnati, OH: Interview, January 10, 1991.

Russell, T. Manager, Continuous Improvement Operation, Aircraft Engines Engineering Division, General Electric Aircraft Division, Cincinnati, OH: Interview, January 10, 1991.

Saylor, M. Corporate Director, Quality Standards and Certification, Cincinnati, OH: Interview, December 14, 1990.

Scherkenbach, W. W. 1991. *The Deming Route to Quality and Productivity, Road Maps and Roadblocks*. Washington, DC: Ceap Press.

Scholtes, P. R. et al. 1989. *The Team Handbook, How to Use Teams to Improve Quality*. Madison, WI: Joiner Associates, Inc.

Sergiovanni, T. 1992. "Why We Should Seek Substitutes for Leadership," *Educational Leadership*, February.

Shewhart, W. A. 1986. *Statistical Method from the Viewpoint of Quality Control*. Washington, DC: Graduate Department of Agriculture (originally published in 1939 by Dover).

Shingo, S. 1986. *Zero Quality Control: Source Inspection and the Poka-Yoke System*. Cambridge, MA: Productivity Press.

1992. "Transforming Leadership," *Educational Leadership* (Feb.):49.

Tribus, M. and Y. Isuda. 1985. "The Quality Imperative in the New Economic Era." Cambridge, MA: Massachusetts Institute of Technology, Center for Advanced Engineering Study.

Walton, M. 1986. *The Deming Management Method*. New York, NY: Dodd, Mead and Co.

Wheeler, D. J. 1990. "Disabling and Enabling Management," *Fourth International Deming User's Group Conference, Cincinnati, OH, August 20–21, 1990*.

Wolfram, K. Director, Consumer Research, The Kroger Company, Cincinnati, OH: Interview, January 7, 1991.

INDEX

ABOUT THE AUTHOR

 Dr. Leo H. Bradley is an Associate Professor of Educational Leadership at Xavier University, Cincinnati, Ohio where he teaches administration, curriculum design, and school law. Prior to coming to Xavier, Dr. Bradley spent thirty years in the Ohio Public School System as teacher, principal, assistant superintendent, and superintendent. He also worked in quality control for the Magnavox Corporation and in manufacturing for Cincinnati Milicron.

This is Dr. Bradley's third book. Previous books are *Curriculum Leadership and Development Handbook*, and *Complete Guide to Competency Based Education*, both published by Prentice-Hall.

In his spare time Dr. Bradley writes songs and baseball literature, both historical and fiction.